A CONCISE DICTIONARY OF ISLAMIC TERMS

A CONCISE DICTIONARY OF ISLAMIC TERMS

Compiled by:
M. A. Qãzi

Revised and enlarged by:
Mohammad Sa'îd El-Dabbãs

KITAB BHAVAN
New Delhi-110002 (India)

Kitab Bhavan
Publishers, Distributors, Exporters & Importers
1784, Kalan Mahal, Darya Ganj
New Delhi - 1100 02 (India)

Phone : (91-11) 23277392/93, 23274686, 30906494
website : www.kitabbhavan.com
Email : nasri@vsnl.com
Fax : (91-11) 23263383

First Edition 2000
IInd Reprinted 2006

ISBN: 81-7151-295-X

Published in India by :
Nusrat Ali Nasri for Kitab Bhavan
1784, Kalan Mahal, Darya Ganj
New Delhi - 1100 02 [India]

Printed in India at :
Nice Printing Press
Khureji Khas, Delhi-110051

PREFACE

This dictionary presents a collection of Islāmic Terms and Names which, in my opinion, are important to the study of Holy Qur'ān and Ḥadīth (sayings and traditions of Prophet Muḥammad S.A.A.W.).

Arabic words, in bold English, are listed alphabetically and according to their pronounciation. The system used in this book for transliteration of these words is listed on page iv. The word in Arabic script is then followed by its exact meaning or an equivalent in the English language, with appropriate references, wherever necessary. Reference books used in the compilation of this work are listed at the end and are recommended for further reading.

This small book has been compiled to satisfy the need of a large number of English reading people, both in this country and abroad, who have become increasingly interested in Islām due to current events, and also due to the fact that it is the only Religion which is Universal and guarantees social, political and economic justice to all human beings, irrespective of their color, race, creed or national origin.

This is a concise dictionary and is not meant to be an encyclopaedia, a biography or a complete reference book on Islām, although it may serve one or all of these purposes in a small way. I pray that may this humble effort also help our Muslim brothers and sisters to read, understand and act upon the teachings of Holy Qur'ān as elucidated by the Prophet S.A.A.W. himself, Āmīn.

I am deeply indebted to my brother in Islām, Mohammad Sa'īd El-Dabbās, who, inspite of his multifarious activities, was able to spare some of his precious time and took great pains in revising and enlarging the original manuscript to make it as comprehensive as it is. May Allāh bless him, Amin.

Last but not least, I am grateful to all those brothers and sisters, both here and overseas, who have encouraged us with helpful advice and constructive criticism. We are also grateful for their continued material, spiritual and moral support in our long struggle in the Way of Allāh. May Allāh reward them all accordingly, Āmīn.

All praises are due to Allāh Alone, Who is my source of inspiration and to Whom I shall return.

M. A. Qāzī
Des Plaines, Ill.

TRANSLITERATION OF ARABIC NAMES

The following system has been used in this book:

Consonant	ا	'a		ط	ṭ
Sound				ظ	ṭh
Long Vovel	آ	ā		ع	'
	ب	b		غ	gh
	ت	t		ف	f
	ث	th		ق	q
	ج	j		ك	k
	ح	ḥ		ل	l
	خ	kh		م	m
	د	d		ن	n
	ذ	th		ه	h
	ر	r		و	w
	ز	z	Long Vovel	و	ū
	س	s	Diphthong	و	au
	ش	sh	Consonant	ى	y
	ص	ṣ	Long Vovel	ى	ī
	ض	ḍ	Diphthong	ى	ai

Fatḥa	ـَـ	Short Vovel	a
Kasra	ـِـ	Short Vovel	i
Dhamma	ـُـ	Short Vovel	u

NOTE

No distinctive sign is used for Hamza (ء).

—A—

'Abd	عبد	A male slave.
'Abad	أبد	Eternity, without end.
'Abraṣ	أبرص	One who is born leprous See H.Q. 3:49.
'Abtar	أبتر	Cut off, without offspring. See H.Q. 108:3.
'Ād	عاد	A tribe of people who lived in the southern part of Arabia after Noah (A.A.). They were prosperous, but haughty and disobedient to Allāh, so He destroyed them with violent, destructive westernly winds.
'Adab	أدب	Discipline of the mind and manners; a mode of conduct or behavior; good education and good breeding, politeness. Also, literature that consists of all types of writing: poetry, prose, etc.
Ad-Dabūr	الدبور	A westernly wind.
'Ad-khar or 'Id-khir	أذخر / إدخر	A kind of grass well known for its good smell, found in Ḥijāz (S.A.) used mainly by blacksmiths.
al-'Ādil	العادل	The just, one of the ninty-nine attributes of Allāh (S.W.)[1]
'Adl	عدل	Justice, equalizing.
'Afū	عفو	Generally used for pardon or forgiveness, means erasing.
al-'Afuww	العفوّ	The forgiver, the oft-pardoning, one of the ninty-nine attributes of Allāh (S.W.)
al-'Aḥad	الأحد	The One, a title of Allāh (S.W.), one of the ninty-nine attributes of Allāh (S.W.)
'Aḥkām	احكام	Orders according to Islāmic law and jurisprudence. There are five kinds of orders or rules: (1) Wājib واجب -Compulsory. (2) Mustaḥabb مستحب -Order without obligation. (3) Muḥarram or Ḥarām محرم أو حرام -Forbidden. (4) Makrūḥ مكروه -Disliked but not forbidden. (5) Ḥalāl حلال -Legal and allowed.

---

[1] (S.W.) Abbreviation used for "Subḥānahū wa ta-'ālā", that means: All glory be to Him nothing matches Him, He is the most high, Allāh. سبحانه تعالى

'Ahl-ul-Bait or Āl-ul-Bait	اهل البيت آل البيت	"The people of the house", Muḥammad's (S.A.A.W.)[2] household.
'Ahl-ul-Kitāb	اهل الكتاب	"The people of the book or scripture", meaning the Jews and Christians.
'Aḥmad	احمد	The name under which Jesus (P.B.U.H.) prophecized the coming of Prophet Muḥammad (S.A.A.W.). Another name for Prophet Muḥammad (S.A.A.W.).
al-'Aḥzāb	الاحزاب	"The confederates", the parties, groups, the title of the 33rd Sūra of the Holy Qurān. Also, a name of an Islāmic battle known as al-Khandaq.
'Ajwah	عجوة	A kind of date.
'Akbar	اكبر	Greatest. A discription used especially with the name of Allāh (S.W.), i.e. Allāh-u-'Akbar.
'Akmah	اكمه	The one who is born blind. See H.Q. al-Baqarah 3:49.
Āl	آل	Used for the offspring of Prophet Muḥammad (S.A.A.W.). It could generally mean the family and relatives.
'Alāmāt-un-Nubuwwah	علامات النبوه	The signs of the prophecy, the miracles of Prophet Muḥammad (S.A.A.W.).
'Alāmāt-us-Sā' ah	علامات الساعة	The signs of the Hour, i.e. the Day of resurrection.
'Alaq	علق	"Congealed blood", the title of Sūra 96 of the Holy Qurān.
'Alf	ألف	One thousand.
al-Ḥamd	الحمد	"Praise", the title of the opening Sūra of the Holy Qurān.
Al-Ḥamdu lil-lāh	الحمد لله	All praises are due to Allāh (S.W.) Alone.
'Alif	ألف	The first letter of the 'Arabic Alphabet, a. It is used quite a few times in the beginning of the various Sūras of the Holy Qurān. However, no one knows what it means there except Allāh (S.W.).

---

[2] S.A.A.W. Abbreviation used for "Ṣall-al-lāhu 'Alihi wa ṣallam", meaning: May the peace and the blessings of Allāh be upon him (Prophet Muḥammad). صلى الله عليه وسلم

Ālu-'Imrān	آل عمران	The family of 'Imrāh, the title of the 3rd Sūra in the Holy Qurān.
al-Ja 'rānah	الجعرانه	A name of a place a few miles from Mecca. The Prophet (S.A.A.W.) distributed the war booties of the battle of Ḥunain there, and from there he assumed the state of 'Iḥrām to perform 'Umrah.
al-Kauthar	الكوثر	The sacred fountain in Paradise, or the abundance. The title of Sūra 108 in the Holy Qurān.
al-Khandaq	الخندق	The trench or the ditch. The name of one of the most well-known Islāmic battles which took place in Shaw-wāl and Thul-Qa'dah of the 5th year A.H. Prophet Muḥammad (S.A.A.W.), himself participated in the battle, and the idea of digging a trench is attributed to Salmān al-Fārisī, may Allāh be pleased with him.
Allāh	الله	God, the Deity.
Allāhu 'Akbar	الله اكبر	Takbīr, Allāh is great, Allāh is the greatest.
'Amah	أمة	A female slave.
'Amat-ul-lāh	أمة الله	The female slave servant of Allāh (S.W.).
Āmīn	آمين	Used at the close of a prayer of Sūra al-Fātiḥah, meaning: "O Allāh! Please accept our invocation."
'Amīn	أمين	Faithful, a title given to young Muḥammad (S.A.A.W.) because of his honesty and truthfulness.
'Amīr-ul-Hajj	اميرالحج	The officer in charge of the pilgrimage to Mecca, usually nominated from among a group of pilgrims to lead them.
'Amīr-ul-M'uminīn	أمير المؤمنين	The commander of the believers, a title given to the Caliph of al-Islām.
'Am-mā ba'du	أمّا بعد	An expression used for separating an introduction from the main topic in a speech; the introduction being usually concerned with Allāh's praises and glorification. Literally it means: "Whatever comes after". Now then . . . ; now on to our topic. . . .
al-'An'ām	الانعام	"The Cattle", the title of the 6th Sūra of the Holy Qurān.

al-'Anfāl	الانفال	"The Spoils of War", the title of the 8th Sūra of the Holy Qurān.
al-'Ankabūt	العنكبوت	"The Spider", the title of the 29th Sūra of the Holy Qurān.
al-'Anṣār	الأنصار	"The Helpers", the companions of the Prophet (S.A.A.W.) from the inhabitants of Medīna, who embraced al-Islām and supported him and who received and entertained the Muslir 'migra from Mecca.
al-'Aqabah	العقبة	A sheltered glen near Minā celebrated as the scene of two pledges of the non-believers at the hands of Prophet Muḥammad (S.A.A.W.).
al-'Aqabat-ul-'Ūlā	العقبة الاولى	The first "sheltered glen" refering to the incide of the first pledge of the unbeliever vith Prophet Muḥammad (S.A.A.W.).
al- Aqabatu-th thāniyah	الثانيه	..e second pledge.
al-'Aqīq	العقيق	A valley about seven (7) kilometers west of Medīna. Also, carnelian, a p ecious natural stone.
'Aqīqah	عقيقـة	A custom obse ne Muslims, leaving the ai on an infant's head until the seventh day when it is shaved and animals are sacrificed (two sheep for a oy and one for a girl).
al-'A'rāf	الاعراف	The partition between Heaven and Hell, the title the 7th Sūra of the Holy Qurān.
Arafāt	عرفات	"The Plain of Recognition", a place situated about 25 kilometers to the east of Mecca, where Pilgrims stay on the 9th day of Thul-Ḥijjah, the 10th month of the Islāmic calendar, recite the Khuṭbah and pray Ṭhuhr and 'Aṣr prayers together at 'Aṣr time as a fulfilment of Ḥajj (Pilgrimage).
'Arāk	أراك	A tree from which Siwāk, the wooden toothbrush, is made.
'Ariḥah	أريحة	A village towards Shām, "Syria."
'Ariyyah Plural-'Arāya	عريّة عرايا	Bai'ul-'Arāya is a kind of sale by which the owner of 'Arāya is allowed to sell the fresh dates while they are still over the palms by means of estimation for dry plucked dates. العرايا

al-'Arsh	العرش	The Throne of Allāh (S.W.).
'Arsh	عرش	Any throne.
'Aṣabah	عصبة	All male relatives of a deceased person, from the father's side.
'Aṣabi-yah	عصبية	Zealous partisanship, tribal solidarity, racialism, clannishness, which al-Islām has forbidden and condemned. It is an emotional, irrational involvement displayed by the narrow-minded tribes.
'Aṣb	عصب	A kind of Yemenī cloth that is very coarse.
'Aṣḥāb	أصحاب	The companions or associates of Prophet Muḥammad (S.A.A.W.).
'Aṣḥāb-ul-'Aikah	أصحاب الأيكة	"The people of the wood," perhaps it is a name of a town or a tract. They are the people of Prophet Shu'aib of Madyan, or a group among them or in their neighbourhood.
'Aṣḥāb-ul-Fīl	أصحاب الفيل	"The companions of the elephant", the title of Sūra 105 of the Holy Qurān.
'Aṣḥāb-uṣ-Ṣuf-fah	أصحاب الصفّة	"The bench sitters," at the Mosque of Medīna. Also known as 'Ahl-uṣ-Ṣuf-fah, the people of Ṣuf-fah, a place known in Medīna.
al-'Asharah-al-Mubash-sharah	العشرة المبشرة	"The ten who received glad tidings," who were foretold that they will reside in Paradise forever and include: 'Abū Bakr, 'Umar, 'Uthmān, 'Alī, Ṭalḥah, az-Zubair, 'Abd-ur-Raḥmān, Sa'd Ibn 'Abī-Waqqāṣ, Sa'īd bin Zaid, Bilāl and 'Abū 'Ubaidah Ibn al-Jar-rāḥ.
'Aṣḥāb-ul-Kahf	أصحاب الكهف	"The companions of the Cave," the title of the 18th Sūra of the Holy Qurān.
'Āshūrā'	عاشوراء	The tenth of the month of Muḥar-ram, i.e. the first month in the Muslim calendar.
'Asmā-ul-lāh	أسماء الله	The names or attributes of Allāh (S.W.).
Al-'Asr	العصر	The afternoon prayer; title of the 103rd Sūra of the Holy Qurān. Also, means the time through the ages.

As-Ṣafā	الصفا	A name of a hill-like elevation in Mecca where Hajar, the wife of Prophet 'Ibrāhīm (A.A.) , walked and ran to the other end which is known as al-Marwah while she was seeking water for her son Ismā'īl (A.A.). It is one of the important Sha'ā'ir (ceremonies and actions) of Ḥajj. Each Pilgrim should observe this and practice it.
As-Ṣaff	الصف	The line, the battle array, the title of Sūra 61 of the Holy Qurān.
'Atarat-un-Nabī	عَترَةُ النبي	The decendants of Prophet Muḥammad (S.A.A.W.). See also: Āl-ul-Bait, 'Ahl-ul-Bait.
'Athāb-ul-Qabr	عذاب القبر	"The Punishment of the Grave," part of the Muslim faith. Prophet Muḥammad (S.A.A.W.) was reported as saying: "O Allāh, I seek refuge with You from the torment of the grave: "Allāhumma in-nī 'A'ūthu bika min 'athābil Qabr."
'Āthān	أذان	The call for prayer.
'Athar	أثر	A trace. In the Islāmic sense, it means a saying or practice traditionally observed by a Ṣaḥābī, a companion of Prophet Muḥammad (S.A.A.W.).
'Athina	أذن	Permitted.
'Athkār	أذكار	Supplications, or preferable prayers that were traditionally practiced by Prophet Muḥammad (S.A.A.W.). These prayers are to be offered at various times and on different occasions.
'A'ūthu Billāh	أعوذ بالله	A Prayer. I seek refuge and protection of Allāh (S.W.).
'Awāl-il-Medīna	عوالى المدينة	Outskirts of al-Medīna at a distance of four or more miles.
al-'Awāmir	العوامر	Snakes living in houses.
'Awāq	أواق	Plural of 'Uqiyah; 5 'Awāq = 22 Riāls "Fransa" Silver.
'Awliyā'	أولياء	Plural of Walī, "Favorites of Allāh (S.W.), i.e. al-Khaḍir, the knowledgable man whom Moses (P.B.U.H.) met and learned from.

[3] A.A, Abbreviation form for " 'Alaih-is-Salām", which means: Peace be upon him. عليه السّلام.

'Awrah	عورة	The part of the body which is unlawfully exposed before others. Also means, unsafe or unprotected.
'Awsuq	أوسق	Plural of "Wasaq", which is a measure equal to 60 Ṣā's. One Ṣā's = 3 kilograms, approx.
'Āyāt	آيات	Signs, proofs, clear evidence or miracles; also verses of the Holy Qurān.
'Āyat-ul-Kursī	آية الكرسى	"The Verse of the Throne," verse 255 of Sūra al-Baqarah of the Holy Qurān.
'Ay-yim	أيّم	A woman having no husband, whether a virgin or a widow.
Āzar	آزر	The father of Prophet Ibrāhīm (A.A.).
al-'Azīz	العزيز	"The Powerful or the Mighty One," one of the ninty-nine attributes of Allāh (S.W.).
'Azlām	أزلام	Literally means "arrows". Here it also means a kind of gambling practiced by pagans to try to forecast the future.
al-'Athīm	العظيم	"The Great One," one of the ninty-nine attributes of Allāh (S.W.).

—B—

Bāb-ur-Rai-yān	باب الريان	One of the eight doors of Paradise which is defined especially for the fasting people, as reported by Prophet Muḥammad (S.A.A.W.).
Bāb-us-Salām	باب السلام	"The Gate of Peace", a gate in the Sacred Mosque at Mecca.
Badanah Plural: Budn	بدنة بدن	A camel offered as a sacrifice.
al-Badī	البديع	"He who originates," one of the ninty-nine attributes of Allāh (S.W.). See H.Q. 2:117, Sūra al-Baqarah.
Badr	بدر	A place about 150 km to the south of Al-Medīna, where the first great battle in Islāmic History took place. The battle was fought between the early Muslims and the infidels of Quraish. Some of the

		Muslim historians refer to it as Badr al-Kubrā, the greatest Badr بدر الكبرى so as to differentiate it from Badr-us-Ṣughrā, the smallest Badr بدر الصغرى. Both of the battles at Badr were named for the source of water located there.
Bahīrah	بَحِيرَة	A milking she-camel who was dedicated to idols or other deities. See H.W. 5:106, al-Mā'idah.
Bai'	بيع	Sale, barter, a commercial deal.
al-Bait-al-Harām	البيت الحرام	"The Sacred House," a name given to the Holy Ka'bah in Mecca.
al-Bā'ith	الباعث	"He who awakes," one of the ninty-nine attributes of Allāh (S.W.).
al-Bait-ul-'Atīq	البيت العتيق	The Oldest House, refering to the Holy Ka'bah. See H.Q. 22:29, al-Ḥajj.
Bait-ul-lāh	بيت الله	"The House of Allāh (S.W.)", another name for the Ka'ba.
al-Bait-ul-Ma'mūr	بيت المعمور	The much-frequented fane - temple, usually understood to mean the Ka'bah. See H.Q. 52:4. Also, "The Inhabited House," Allāh's house in the Seventh Heaven.
Bait-ul-Maqdis	بيت المقدس	"The Holy House", the famous Mosque in Jerusalem which is regarded as the third greatest mosque in the Islāmic World, the first and second being al-Masjid al-Ḥarām in Mecca, and the Mosque of Prophet Muḥammad (S.A.A.W.) at al-Medīna, respectively.
al-Bai-y'ān	البيعان	The seller and the buyer. This 'Arabic word includes both of the above.
al-Bai-yinah	البيّنة	"The Clear Evidence," the title of the 98th Sūra of the Holy Qurān.
Balam	بلم	Ox.
Ban-ūl-'Aysār	بنوالأيسار	The Byzantines.
Banū 'Isrā'īl	بنواسرائيل	The children of Israēl, the Jews, a title of the 17th Sūra of the Holy Qurān.
Banū Jadīlah	بنوجديلة	The name of the palace of Caliph Mu'āwiya at al-Medīna.

al-Bāqī	الباقي	"He who remains", one of the ninty-nine attributes of Allāh (S.W.).
al-Baqī'	البقيع	The cemetary of the peole of al-Medīna where many of the companions and members of the family of the Prophet Muḥammad (S.A.A.W.) are buried.
al-Baqarah	البق	"The Cow," the title of the second Sūra of the Ho- Qurān
		mmunity or Security", the title of the 9th Sūra of .e Holy Qurān. Also means innocence.
Baraka		To make a camel kneel down.
Bāraka	بارَك	To bless.
Barakah	بَرَكَة	Blessing.
Barī	بريء	Innocent.
Al-Bārī'	البارئ	"The Maker, the Creator," one of the ninty-ni attributes of Allāh (S.W.).
Bārnabās	برنابا	One of the Apostles of Jesus, in whose Gospel the forthcoming prophethood of Muḥammad (S.A.A.W.) was prophecized by Jesus (A.A.).
Bar	برّ	Pious, reverent. It is used in connection with establishing good relations with the parents.
al-Barr	البرّ	"The Beneficent One", one of the ninty-nine attributes of Allāh, (S.W). Also means: the land as opposed to the sea
Barra	برّ	To be pious, or reverent an evoted, dutiful, upright.
al-Baṣīr	البصير	"The All-Seeing One", one of th -nine attributes of Allāh (S.W.).
al-Bāsiṭ	الباسط	"He who spreads," one of the ninty-nine attributes of Allāh (S.W.).
Batar	بتر	To cut off.
Ba'th	بعث	Sending out, emission, delegation, resurrection enaissance. Yawm-ul-Ba'th يوم البعث the Day of Resurrection, Judgement.

Bathaq بثق
A kind of alcoholic drink made from grapes.

Bāṭil باطل
Falsehood, a false doctrine.

al-Bāṭin الباطن
"The Hidden or Concealed One," one of the ninty-nine attributes of Allāh (S.W.).

Batūl بتول
A virgin, a branch cut from a palm tree or birch tree. Also, it is a title that accompanies the name of Lady Virgin Mary (A.A.).

Bid'ah بدعة
An innovation in religio

Bint Labūn بنت لبون
A one year old she-can

B'ir بئر
A well.

Birr برّ
Piety, righteousness. See H.Q. 2:177.

B'iru Zam-Zam بئر زمزم
The well-known well of Zam-Zam in the Sacred Mosque in Mecca.

Bism-il-lāh بسم الله
"In or with the name of Allāh," used before commencement of any work, etc.

Bi'thah بعثه
Mission. When this word is used in relation to the prophets and messengers, it means that they have been entrusted with the Mission of propagating the Dīn, the religion of truth from Allāh (S.W.); they are 'chosen' for the office of prophethood.

Bu'āth بُعاث
A place about two miles from al-Medīna where a battle took place between the 'Anṣārī tribes of al-'Aws and the al-Khazraj before the advent of al-Islām.

Budn بُدن
Plural of Badanah, the fat camels. See H.Q. 22:36.

Buhtān بُهتان
A false accusation, calumny, slander.

Buraiḥah بريحة
One of 'Abū Ṭalḥa's gardens situated opposite the Prophet's Mosque in Mecca where Allāh's Apostle (S.A.A.W.) used to go to sit in its shade and drink fresh water.

Burāq بُراق
"The Bright One". an animal-like, bigger than a donkey and smaller than a horse on which Prophet Muḥammad (S.A.A.W.) went for the 'Isrā' (journey during the night).

Burdah	بُرْدَه	A cloak, garment. Prophet Muḥammad (S.A.A.W.), used to wear it as an outer garment.
Burnus	برنس	A hooded cloak.
Burqu'	بُرقُع	A black square narrow dress, covering sheet, veil worn by Muslim women.
Burr	برّ	Wheat.
Burūd	برود	A distance of 16 Farsakhs.
Burūdun Yamāni-yah	برود يمانية	Yemeni garments, well-known garments fo their make and quality.
Burūj	بروج	"Towers", signs of the Zodiac, the title of the 85th Sūra of the Holy Qurān.
Bushrā	بشرىٰ	"Good News", used for spreading good tidings.
Buthā	بطحان	A valley in al-Medīna.

—D—

Dabūr	دبور	Westernly wind.
Daghābis	دغابس	A kind of cucumber, same as Qith-thā'.
-Dahr	الدهر	"The Man or A Long Space of Time," the title of the 76th Sūra of the Holy Qurān.
Dajal	دجل	False, lying, cheating, deceiving.
Daj-jāl	دجال	Swindler, cheat, imposter. In reference to a false messiah to come after Prophet Muḥammad (S.A.A.W.), and mislead the people. In al-Islām, Prophet Muḥammad (S.A.A.W.) reported that he sought refuge with Allāh (S.W.) from the Daj-jāl: O Allāh! I seek refuge with you from the test of the false messiah. (Allāhumma 'innī 'a-'ūthu bika min fitna-til-masīḥ-id-daj-jāl). اللّهم انى اعوذبك من فتنة المسيح الدجال
Dalīl	دليل	An arguement, proof, evidence. Also means guide.
Dāniq	دانق	A coin equal in value to one sixth of a Dirham. A coin equal in value to a penny
Dār	دار	A house, dwelling, land, country.

Darajah	درجه	Position, step. See H.Q. 2:228.
Dark	درن	Bottom. See H.Q. 4:145.
Dār-ul-Islām	دارالاسلام	A Muslim country run strictly according to the laws of Qurān and Sunnah.
Da'wa	دعوىٰ	A claim, allegation, law suit, case.
D'awah	دعوة	Call, appeal, invocation, invitation, missionary activity, supplication, propogation of al-Islām.
Dībaj	ديباج	A kind of silken cloth.
Dīn	دين	Religion brought by the Prophets of Allāh (S.W.).
Dīnār	دينار	Islāmic currency of gold of one Mithqāl weight equal to about 10 shillings or one dollar.
Dirham	درهم	Islāmic silver currency weighing about 50 grains of barley.
Di-yah	دية	Compensation paid by the killer to the relatives of the victim in unintentional cases of death, usually fixed by the government.
Du'ā	دُعاء	Supplication, prayer, invocation to Allāh (S.W.).
Du'ā'ul-Qunūt	دُعاءالقنوت	Prayer said standing, usually after reciting al-Fātiḥa and al-'Ikhlāṣ in the third Rak'a of the "Witr" prayer, the odd numbers of Rak'āt after 'Ishā'.
Dubbā	دباء	The name of a pot in which alcoholic drinks used to be prepared.
Dubur	دبر	Back or flee, run away. See Holy Qurān 54:45.
Duḥā	ضحىٰ	Forenoon, the title of the 93rd Sūra of the Holy Qurān.
ad-Dukhān	الدخان	"The Smoke", the title of the 44th Sūra of the Holy Qurān.
Duldul	دلدل	The name of Prophet Muḥammad's mule, which he gave as a gift to 'Alī (R.A.A.).

—F—

Fadak	فدك	A town near al-Medīna.
Fāḥish	فاحش	One who talks evil, or any evil talk.
Fāḥishah	فاحشة	Atrocity, wrong deed. See H.Q. 3:135.
Faḥshā'	فحشاء	Vile deed, shameful. See H.Q. 29:45.
Faī'	فئ	War booty gained from infidels without fighting.
Fajr (al-Fajr)	فجر (الفجر)	Dawn, early morning before sunrise, the title of the 89th Sūra of the Holy Qurān.
Fā'l	فال	A good omen, sign, optimistic out-look.
al-Falaq	الفلق	"The Day-Break", the title of the 113th Sūra of the Holy Qurān.
Faqīh	فقيه	An Islāmic learned man, a lawyer or theologian who can give religious verdicts.
Far'	فرع	The first born of an animal, offered as a sacrifice to idols by the pagans.
Farā'id	فرائد	Shares fixed for the relatives of a deceased which are fixed and described in the H.Q. 4:11, 12 and 76
ard, Farīḍah **Pl.-Farā'iḍ**	فرض، فريضة فرائض	An enjoining or obligatory duty to Allāh (S.W.).
arsakh	فرسخ	A distance of three (3) miles. One (1) mile = 5280 ft. or 1760 yards.
Fāsid	فاسد	A seditious or rebellious person.
Fāsiq	فاسق	A reprobate person, neglectful and careless in his dress and behaviour whose evidence is not admissable in the case of witnessing.
Fatāt	فتاة	A female slave.
al-Fatḥ	الفتح	"The Victory", the title of the 48th Sūra in the Holy Qurān.
al-Fātiḥah	الفاتحة	"The Opening One", the first Sūra of the Holy Qurān.

al-Fat-tāḥ	الفتاح	"The opener", one of the ninty-nine attributes of Allāh (S.W.).
Fatwā	فتوىٰ	A religious verdict pronounced by the K͟halīfah, the Muftī or the Qāḍī or a Faqīh, the learned person of a place or of a particular time.
Fidyah or Fidā'	فدية فدىٰ	A ransom, compensation for ceremonies missed or wrongly practiced; usually in the form of money, food-stuff or sacrifice.
al-Fīl	الفيل	"The Elephant", the title of the 105th Sūra of the Holy Qurān.
Fiqh	فقه	Islāmic Jurisprudence. Especially used in regard to law and applications.
al-Firdous	الفردوس	The middle, the last and the highest part of Paradise.
Fuḥs͟h	فحشىٰ	Atrocity, obscene languag
al-Furqān	الفرقان	"Victory on the Day of Badr". the title [illegible]a 25 of the Holy Qurān. Also means proof. evidence. One of the names given to the Hol Qurān.

—G

al-G͟hābah	الغابة	The forest, a well-known place near al-Medina
G͟hadab	غضب	Anger, wrath of Allāh (S.W.).
G͟hadbān	غضبان	Angry. See H.Q. 7:150
G͟hāḍ-ḍa	غضّ	To cast down, lower one's eyes, one's glance out of modesty. See H.Q. 24:30.
G͟hafar	غفر	Pardoned, forgiven. See H.Q. 28:16.
al-G͟haf-fār	الغفار	The same as al-G͟hafūr.
al-G͟hafūr	الغفور	Oft-forgiving, one of the ninty-nine attributes of Allāh (S.W.).
al-G͟haī'	الغئي	Trespassing, transgression, temptation. See H.Q. 2:256.
G͟haib	غيب	Absence, concealed, invisible. An essential part of a Muslim's faith. See H.Q. 2:3.

Ghairah or Ghīrah	غيرة	Jealousy as regards to women, a feeling of great fury, anger when one's prestige and honor is injured or challenged.
Ghaith	غيث	Rain, abundant. See H.Q. 31:34.
Ghaiṭh	غيض	The anger, wrath. See H.Q. 3:119.
al-Ghanī	الغـني	"The Independent One," one of the ninty-nine attributes of Allāh (S.W.).
Gharām	غرام	Love. Penalty, fine. See H.Q. 25:65
al-Gharār	الغرار	The sale of what is not present, i.e. fish that is not caught yet.
al-Ghargharah	الغرغرة	The gurgle. The sounds of the person in the last minutes or seconds of life.
al-Ghārimīn	الغارمـين	Those who are in bondage, literally and figuratively. See H.Q. 9:60.
al-Gharūr	الغرور	Deceptive, delusive. Also, one of the names of Satan. See H.Q. 31:33.
al-Ghāshiyah	الغاشية	"The Covering, Overwhelming", the title of the 88th Sūra of the Holy Qurān.
Ghasaq	غسق	Dusk, dark of night. See H.Q. 17:78
al-Ghasīl	الغسيل	"The Washed". The companion of Prophet Muḥammad (S.A.A.W.), Ḥanthalah, the 'Anṣārian, may Allāh be pleased with him, was known as such because he went to the battle after the first night of his marriage and did not have time to make Ghusl (abulution). The Prophet (S.A.A.W.) said that the angels are washing the soul of Ḥanthalah between the heaven and the earth.
Ghash-sha	غش	Deceive, cheat or act dishonestly.
Ghas-sāqa	غساق	A name of the materials that disbelievers will eat in the Hell fire. See H.Q. 78:25.
Ghauth	غوث	Aid, to appeal for help or one who can cry for help.
Ghāzī	غازي	A hero, warrior, one who fights for the cause of Allāh (S.W.), and is victorious.

Ghazwah, Pl-Ghazwāt غزوة غزوات — A holy battle in the cause of Allāh (S.W.), consisting of large units with the Prophet (S.A.A.W.), himself leading the army.

Ghībah غيبة — Slander, calumny, something uttered in a person's absence, backbiting.

Ghishāwah غشاوة — Cover, veil. See H.Q. 2:7.

Ghislīn غسلين — The name of the materials that the disbelievers will eat in the Hell fire. See H.Q. 69:36.

Ghulūl غلول — Defrauding or stealing from the war booty before distribution.

Ghuraf غرف — Special abode. See H.Q. 39:20.

al-Ghur-r-ul-Muhaj-jalūn الغرّالمحجلون — A name that will be given on the Day of Resurrection to the Muslims because of the parts of their bodies that they used to wash in ablution will glitter at that time.

al-Ghurūr الغرور — Deception, delusion, illusion. See H.Q. 4:120.

Ghusl غسل — Taking a bath in a religious, ceremonial way. This is necessary for one who is Junub (one who has the big impurity, such as, having legal, lawful sexual relations; one who has had a wet dream for both the male and female or for the ending of the period of menstruation for women.)

Ghusl Masnūn غسل مسنون — Washing which is Sunnah, those which Prophet Muḥammad (S.A.A.W.) used to practice; i.e. on Jum'ah (Friday), 'Īds, upon coming back from a journey, etc.

—H—

Ḥabal-al-Ḥabla حبل الحبلة — A kind of sale practiced in the pre-Islāmic ignorant period. One would pay the price of a she-camel which was not yet born, but would be born by the immediate offspring of an expectant she-camel.

Ḥaḍānah حضانة — A person other than a parent who had charge of a child and carried him/her, rearing of fostering them.

Ḥadath حدث — (A) Small Ḥadath - Passing gas or urine, answering the call of nature. (B) Big Ḥadath - Sexual discharge, wet dreams, the menstruation period of women.

Ḥadd Pl-Ḥudūd	حدّ ، حدود	Limits imposed by Allāh (S.W.) throught Prophet Muḥammad (S.A.A.W.), which are mentioned in the Holy Qurān or in Ḥadīth. See Tā'thīr.
Hadī	هدى	An animal offered as a sacrifice.
al-Ḥadīd	الحديد	"Iron," the title fo the 57th Sūra of the Holy Qurān.
Ḥadīth Pl-'Aḥādīth	حديث ـ احاديث	The traditions of the Prophet (S.A.A.W.), i.e. his sayings.
Ḥadīth Qudsī	حديث قدسي	A divine saying. A term used for a Ḥadīth which relates a revelation from Allāh in the language of Prophet Muḥammad (S.A.A.W.).
Ḥafaṭhah	حفظة	An appellation of the Recording Angels who write down the actions of the sons of Adam (A.A.), or the entire mankind.
Ḥāfiṭh al-Ḥāfiṭh	حافظ الحافظ	One who has committed the complete Qurān to memory. Also, one of the ninty-nine attributes of Allāh (S.W.). See H.Q. 86:4.
Ḥaiḍ	حيض	Menstruation, Menses.
Ḥāi'ḍ	حائض	A menstruating woman.
Ḥais	حيس	A dish made of cooking-butter, dates and cheese.
al-Ḥaiyy	الحي	"The Living One," one of the ninty-nine attributes of Allāh (A.W.).
al-Ḥajar-ul-'Aswad	الحجرالاسود	"The Black Stone," embedded in one of the Yemenite (southern) corners of the Holy Ka'ba in Mecca.
Ḥājj	حاج	A person who has performed the Ḥajj, a Pilgrim to Mecca.
Ḥajj	حج	One of the five pillars of al-Islām, a pilgrimage to Mecca is obligatory on every Muslim who can afford it at least once in his lifetime. Also, Ḥajj is the title of the 22nd Sūra of the Holy Qurān.
Ḥajj-ul-'Akbar	حج الاكبر	The Day of Naḥr, the 10th day of Thul-Ḥijjah.

Ḥajjat-ul-Wadā‘	حجة الوداع	The last or farewell pilgrimage performed by the Prophet (S.A.A.W.).
Ḥajj-ul-'Aṣghar	حج الأصغر	‘Umra, pilgrimage any time of the year except in the month of Thul-Ḥijjah.
Ḥajj-ul-Qirān	حج القران	Ḥajj performed along with ‘Umra and keeping the state of 'Iḥrām for both.
Ḥajjun-Mabrūr	حج امبرور	Accepted pilgrimage by Allāh (S.W.), one that has been performed perfectly according to the Prophet's traditions.
Ḥajju-t-Tamattu‘	حج المتمتع	Performing ‘Umra before Ḥajj while assuming 'Iḥrām separately for each.
al-Ḥakīm	الحكيم	"The Wise One," one of the ninty-nine attributes of Allāh (S.W.).
Ḥalāl	حلال	Lawful, permissible, legal, sacrificed with the name of Allāh.
al-Ḥalīm	الحليم	"The Patient," one of the ninty-nine attributes of Allāh (S.W.).
Ḥal-la	حل	Befalled, became due. See H.Q. 20:81.
Ḥamā'	حما	Fetid mud mixed with black. Also, a certain plant that grows in Najd in the sands and in plain or soft land. See H.Q. 15:26.
Ḥamālah	حمالة	Compensation for murder or manslaughter.
al-Ḥamd	الحمد	"The Praise."
Ḥami'ah	حمئة	A well or spring foul with black, fetid mud. See H.Q. 18:86
al-Ḥamīd	الحميد	"The Laudable," the one worthy of praise, one of the ninty-nine atributes of Allāh (S.W.).
al-Ḥamīyah	الحمية	The chauvinism, a kind of strong temperament among the tribal people.
Ḥanafī	حنفي	A follower of the sect or school of thought of Emām 'Abū Ḥanīfah.
Ḥanafi-yah	حنفية	The persons called in relation to the Emām 'Abū Ḥanīfah because they hold his tenets. An inclining

		to a thing, or actually to the law of 'Ibrāhīm (A.A.), which is the religion of al-Islām.
Ḥanīf	حنيف	"One who is Inclined." Worshipping Allāh (S.W.) alone and nothing else along with Him or associating no partners with Him, One who is of the religion of 'Ibrāhim (A.A.), See H.Q. 3:67.
Ḥanīth	حنيذ	Meat roasted by having stones put upon it to cook it thoroughly. See H.Q. 11:69.
al-Ḥaqq	الحق	"The Truth," one of the ninty-nine attributes of Allāh (S.W.)
al-Ḥāq-qah	الحاقة	"The Surely Impending or The Reality," the title of the 69th Sūra of the Holy Qurān.
Ḥaraj	حرج	Killing, critical situation.
Ḥaram	حرم	Sacred, sanctuary of Mecca or al-Medīna.
Ḥarām	حرام	Prohibited, unlawful, forbidden and punishable from the viewpoint of al-Islām.
Ḥaras	حرس	Guards, protectors. See H.Q. 72:8.
Ḥarb	حرب	War, fight. See H.Q. 2:279.
Ḥarbah	حربة	A short spear.
Ḥarīm	حريم	The female section in a Muslim household.
Ḥarūrā'	حروراء	A town in 'Irāq.
al-Ḥar-rah	الحرة	Land covered with black stones, well-known in al-Medīna.
Ḥasad	حسد	Envy, grudge.
al-Ḥaṣbah or al-Ḥaṣbā'	الحصبة الحصباء	A place outside Mecca where the pilgrims go after finishing all of the ceremonies of Ḥajj.
Ḥaṣḥaṣa	حصحص	Now the truth has become established. See H.Q. 12:51.
Ḥashr	حشر	Gathering, assembling. When Ḥashr is used with the word Yawm (day), it means the Day of Judgement or the Day of Congregation. Yawm-ul-Ḥashr.

al-Ḥāsib or al-Ḥasīb	الحاسب الحسيب	"The Reckoner," one of the ninty-nine attributes of Allāh (S.W.)
Ḥasīr	حسير	A mat that is made from the leaves of the date-palm and is as long or longer as a man's statue.
Hasīs	حسيس	The Sound of Jahannam, "Hell Fire."
Ḥawārī	حواري	The Apostle of Jesus (A.A.), or the disciple.
Hawāzin	هوازن	A tribe of Quraish.
Ḥawbah	حوبة	Maternal tenderness of heart, anxiety, poverty, indigence. Prophet Muḥammed (S.A.A.W.) saying: To thee I make known my want, "ḥawbatī."
Hāwiyah	هاوية	A section of the Hell Fire.
Ḥawl	حول	One complete year.
Ḥawqalah	حوقلة	Signifies the lack of ability to exercise the veneral faculty or being weary and weak. Also signifies saying: "There is no might, no power but with Allāh (S.W.). "Lā ḥawla walā Quw-wata 'il-lā bil-lāh."
Ḥayā'	حياء	Shame, prudency modesty, self-respect, bashfulness.
Hibah	هبة	A deed of gift, a transfer of property made im mediately and without any exchange.
Hidāyah	هداية	Guidance, showing the right path.
Ḥijāb	حجاب	Partition or curtain, veiling or concealing.
Ḥijāz	حجاز	A barrier, partition or separation. A territory in Saūdī Arabia that separates Najd from Tihāmah.
al-Ḥijr	الحجر	Territory between al-Medīna and Syria where the tribe of Thamūd dwelt; the unroofed portion of the Ka'ba which, at present, is in the form of a compound towards the north-west side.
Hijrah	هجرة	Migration, the Muslim era calendar, fleeing from sin. The Muslim era calendar is recorded from the year of the migration of Prophet Muḥammad (S.A.A.W.), from Mecca to al-Medīna.
Hilab	هلب	A kind of scent, perfume.

Hilāl	هلال	The new moon, crescent.
Ḥilf or Half	حلف	An oath, a vow, an affidavit. Also, the act of confederating or making a compact or confederacy, to aid or assist in making an agreement. But this meaning afterwards said to be tropical, when the object of this in the time of paganism was to aid in sedition or the like and in fighting and incursions into the territories of enemies. It was forbidden by Prophet Muḥammad (S.A.A.W.), but when the object was to aid the wronged or for making close the ties of a relationship and the like, he confirmed it.
Ḥilf-ul-Fuḍūl	حلف الفضول	An agreement that took place among the tribes of Arabs before the mission of Prophet Muḥammad (S.A.A.W.), and he himself had participated in it.
Ḥilm	حلم	Gentleness, mildness, clemency, forbearance.
Ḥimā	حمى	Guarded, forbidden A pre-Islāmic institution by which the chief of a tribe took a pasture for his animals preventing others from grazing their animals on it, while he could graze his animal in other's pastures. Al-Islām cancelled such an institution and allowed it only for Zakāt animals.
Him-mah	همّة	Resolution, ability, strength.
Himyān	هميان	A kind of belt part of which serves as a purse to keep money in.
Ḥin-nā' or Ḥin-nah	حنّاء - حنّة	A kind of plant used for dyeing hair, skin, etc, known as Lawsonia intermis or Egyptian privet
Ḥinth	حنث	Violation, or failure to perform an oath. See H Q. 56:46.
Ḥiqqah	حقة	A she-camel that is three years old.
Ḥirā'	حراء	The name of a mountain in which is the well-known cave of Ḥirā', near Mecca where Prophet Muḥammad (S.A.A.W.), was given the first revelation from Allāh (S.W.), by the angel, Jibril (A.A.).
Ḥirṣ	حرص	Eagerness, greed, avarice.
Ḥisāb	حساب	Account When used with the Yawm-ul-Ḥisāb or the Day of Account, it refers to the Day of Judgement.

Hiss	حس	Sense, understanding, feeling.
Hit-tah	حطّة	Alleviation, humiliation. See H.Q. 2:58.
Hizb	حزب	Party, group.
Houriyah	حورية	A very fair woman created by Allāh (S.W.), as such not from the offspring of Adam with their intense black irises of the eyes and their intense white sclera.
Hūb	حوب	Sin or crime, the act of committing a sin or crime, to do what is unlawful. See H.Q. 4:2
Hūbah	حوبة	A weak woman, a weak person, a man who can neither profit nor harm. Prophet Muḥammad (S.A.A.W.), says: "Fear you Allāh (S.W.), with respect to the needy women, who cannot do without someone to maintain them and take constant care of them."
Hubal	هبل	The great idol over the Ka'ba or within it in the pre-Islāmic period.
Hublā	حبلى	A kind of desert tree. A pregnant woman
Ḥubs	حبس	Any bequest for pious purposes.
Hudā	هدى	Guidance. A female name.
Ḥudā'	حداء	Chanting of the camel drivers to keep their camels to a walk.
al-Ḥudaibiyah	الحديبية	A well-known open space ten miles from Mecca on the way to Jeddah, famous for the truce between the Muslims and the Quraish.
Ḥudūd	حدود	Plural of Ḥad. Allāh's boundary limits for Halāl and Harām.
Ḥuj-jah	حجة	A proof, an argument, evidence.
Ḥujrah	حجرة	The chamber of Prophet Muḥammad (S.A.A.W.), where he is buried.
al-Ḥujurāt	الحجرات	"The Chambers," the title of the 49th Sūra of the Holy Qurān.
Ḥukm	حكم	A judgement or a legal decision by Allāh (S.W.). Order or command.

Ḥulm	حلم	A dream. When someone is said to have reached the age of Ḥulm, it means that he has attained puberty or virility in the absolute sense. See H.Q. 24:58.
al-Humazah	الهمزة	"The Slanderer," the title of the 104th Sūra of the Holy Qurān.
Ḥums	حمّس	The tribe of Quraish. Their offspring and their allies were called "Ḥums." This word implies enthusiasm and strictness. The "Ḥums" used to say: "We are the people of Allāh," they thought themselves superior to other people.
Ḥunain	حُنين	A valley between Mecca and Ṭā'if where the Quraish pagans were defeated by Prophet Muḥammad (S.A.A.W.), and his army. See H.Q. 9:25.
Ḥunūṭ	حُنوط	A kind of scent used for embalming the dead.
Ḥūr	حور	Plural of "Ḥūriyah," the women of Paradise described in the Holy Qurān.
Ḥusūm	حسوم	Fatal, grueling. The "fatal nights" are the nights that cut off good and prosperity. See H.Q. 69:7.
Ḥūt	حوت	A fish, any great fish, whale. Also a sign of the Zodiac. The Man of Ḥūt refers to a surname of Prophet Jonah. See H.Q. 68:48.
al-Ḥuṭamah	الحطمة	A section of Hell. To break into pieces. Also, one of the names given to the Hell-Fire. See H.Q. 104:4.

—I—

'Ibādah	عبادة	Worship.
'Iblīs	ابليس	Devil, Satan.
'Īd	عيد	Festival, a happy day, celebration.
'Īdān	عيدان	The two 'Īds: 'Īd-ul-'Aḍḥā and 'Īd-ul-Fiṭr.
'Id-dah	عِدّة	Number, the amount of time that must elapse before a Muslim woman can remarry following a divorce or the death of her husband.

'Idhkhir	إذخِر	A kind of grass well known for its good smell, found in Ḥijāz in Saūdī 'Arabia. It is used primarily by the blacksmiths.
'Īd-ul-'Aḍḥā	عيد الأضحى	The four-day festival of the Muslims starting on the 10th day of the month of Thul-Ḥijjah.
'Īd-ul-Fiṭr	عيد الفطر	The three-day festival of the Muslims starting on the first day of the month of Shaw-wāl, the month following Ramaḍān. Fiṭr literally means "breaking the fast." The Muslims fast during the whole month of Ramaḍān, the ninth month of the Muslim calendar, then when Shaw-wāl comes, they break their fasts.
'Ifṭār	افطار	Breaking the fast.
'Iḥdād	إحداد	The period of mourning the death of a husband, which is four months and ten days.
'Iḥrām	إحرام	Prohibiting. A state in which one is prohibited to practise certain deeds that are lawful at other times. The ceremonies of Ḥajj and 'Umra are performed during such state. When one assumes the state of 'Iḥrām, the first thing one should do is to express mentally and orally one's intention to assume this state for the purpose of performing Ḥajj and 'Umra. Then Talbiya is recited; two sheets of unstitched cloth will be the only clothes that the Muslim male will wear, one around his waist and the other on his left shoulder going around the waist from under the right arm.
'Ihsān	احسان	To confer favors or to perform an action in perfect form. The highest form or level of worship. When you worship Allāh (S.W.), as if you see Him and if you cannot acheive this attitude, you worship Him bearing in mind that He sees you at all times.
'Iḥtilām	احتلام	Noctural emission after which Ghusl is absolutely necessary.
'Ījāb	ايجاب	The first proposal by bargaining parties, acceptance of a marriage.
'Ijl	عجل	Calf. See H.Q. 7:148.
'Ijmā'	إجماع	Collecting or assembling. Unanimous consent of the learned men of al-Islām. It is one of the major sources of Islāmic Jurisprudence.

'Ijtihād	اجتهاد	Exertion. A logical deduction of a learned man of al-Islām. It, also, is one of the major sources of Islāmic Jurisprudence, known also as Ar-Rāi' which means Opinion.
'Īlā'	إيلاء	A form of voluntary, temporary divorce where a husband takes an oath that he will not approach his wife for a certain period of time.
'Ilāh	إله	An object of worship, a god, a deity.
'Ilḥād	إلحاد	Apostasy, hetrodoxy, heresy.
'Ilhām	إلهام	Inspiration from Allāh (S.W.).
'Iliy-yūn	عِلّيّون	The seventh stage of celestial bliss, register of good deeds.
'Ilm	عِلم	The knowledge, preferably religious.
'Ilqā'	إلقاء	Injecting. Teaching of the heart by the power of Allāh (S.W.).
'Īlyā'	ايلياء	Jerusalem.
'Imām	امام	A responsible, knowledgable leader. The person who leads the others in a prayer or a Muslim Caliph.
'Īmān	إيمان	Faith, belief.
al-'Infiṭār	الانفطار	"The Cleaving Asunder," the title of the 82nd Sūra of the Holy Qurān.
'Injibāniyah or Menjibaniyah	عنجبانيه منجبانيه	A woolen garment without marks.
'Injīl	إنجيل	The Bible. Revelation to Jesus from Allāh (S.W.) through Jibrīl (A.A.).
al-'Insān	الإنسان	"The Man," the title of the 76th Sūra of the Holy Qurān.
'Inshā'Allāh-u-Ta'āla	إن شاء الله تعالى	"If it should please Almighty Allāh (S.W.)." Used as an expression for all future, expected happenings or promises made by most Muslims.
al-'Inshirāḥ	الانشراح	"Expanding," the title of the 94th Sūra of the Holy Qurān.

'Iqāmah	إقامة	"Causing to stand." The statements of 'Āth̲ān are recited, reduced, so that the statements that are repeated twice in 'Āth̲ān are recited once in the 'Iqāmah with the exception of the last occurance of Allāh-u-'Akbar. The prayer is offered immediately after 'Iqāmah has been pronounced.
'Iqāmat-uṣ-Salāt	إقامة الصلاة	The offering of the prayers perfectly. This is not understood by many Muslims. It means that: (A) All members of a family or a group, etc. of a town or a village, must offer the prayers, all males in the mosque for the five congregational prayers and the females in their houses, both young and old, from seven years of age up-wards (with no member of the family is excused) at the five fixed stated hours for the five compulsory prayers. If any member intentionally did not offer the prayer, then even if the others prayed, they did not offer the prayer dutifully and perfectly. Each chief of a family or a town or village, etc., is responsible before Allāh (S.W.). (B) to offer the prayer in a way just as Prophet Muḥammad (S.A.A.W.), offered with all its ceremonies, rules and regulations.
Ish̲ā	عِشَاء	The Night Prayer, the time for which starts about one and one half hour after sunset.
Ishtimāl-us-Samā'	اشتمال السماء	The wearing of clothes in two ways: (1) To cover one shoulder with a garment leaving the other shoulder bare; and, (2) To wrap oneself in a garment while sitting in such a way that nothing of that garment would cover one's private parts.
'Islām	إسلام	Submission or resignation to the will of Allāh (S.W.), completely.
'Ism-ul-'A'ṭham	الاسم الأعظم	Exalted Name of Allāh known only to the Prophets.
'Isrāfīl	إسرافيل	The Archangel who will sound the trumpet on the Day of Judgement. One of the four major angels.
'Istabraq	استبرق	Thick dībāj; pure, silken cloth.
'Istibrā'	استبراء	Purification of the womb, period of the month. Also, purification of the urine.
'Istighfār	استغفار	Seeking forgiveness of Allāh (S.W.). Seeking Allāh's pardon.

'Istiḥāḍah	استحاضه	Vaginal bleeding of a women between her regular periods.
'Istikhārah	استخاره	"Asking favors." Seeking Allāh (S.W.) to guide one to the right path or the right sort of action concerning an important endeavour or decision. A two Rak'āt prayer at night or at any other time is offered for this purpose and certain formulae of invocations are read after that.
'Istinjā'	استنجاء	Abstension, cleaning of the private parts after the call of nature with not less than three handfuls of water or dry earth, using the left hand only.
'Istisqā'	استسقاء	Invoking Allāh (S.W.), with two Rak'āt prayer for rain in seasons of drought.
'I'tikāf	اعتكاف	Seclusion in a mosque during the last ten days of Ramaḍān for the purpose of worshipping Allāh (S.W.), only. The one in such a state should not have sexual relations with his wife, and one is not allowed to leave the mosque, except for a very short period of time and only for very special or urgent purposes, i.e., answering the call of nature, for taking meals, to join a funeral procession, etc.
'Izār	إزار	A sheet worn below the waist as part of 'Iḥrām. (See 'Iḥrām).
'Izrā'īl	عزرائيل	The Angel of Death, Malak-ul-Maut. One of the four main defined angels in al-Islām.

— ج —

al-Jab-bār	الجبّار	"The Absolute", one of the ninty-nine attributes of Allāh (S.W.).
Jābī	جابي	A collector of Zakāt or Ṣadqah who is appointed by the State in an Islāmic government.
Jad'ah	جدعة	A four year old she-camel.
Jadd	جَدّ	Paternal or maternal grandfather.
Jahan-nam	جهنّم	Hell, the Hell-fire.
Jāhily-yah	جاهلية	A state of ignorance. The pre-Islāmic era is known as such. See H.Q. 3:154.
Jaḥīm	جحيم	One of the names of the Hell Fire. See H.Q. 2:119.

Jahl	جهل	Ignorance.
Jahr	جهر	Out-loud, reciting out-loud, openly. See H.Q. 16:75.
Jaish-ul-'Usrah	جيش العُسرة	The Muslim army at the battle of Tabūk which was provided with all of the needed provisions by 'Uthmān (R.A.A.). See Tabūk.
Jald	جَلْد	Stripping or whipping. See H.Q. 24:2.
al-Jalīl	الجليل	Lofty, exalted. One of the ninty-nine attributes of Allāh (S.W.). Also, a kind of good smelling grass grown in Mecca.
Jālūt	جالوت	Goliath. See H.Q. 2:249.
Jam'	جمع	Al-Muzdalifah, a small town close to Mecca. The pilgrims should spend the night there after visiting 'Arafāt.
Jamā'ah	جماعة	Congregation, group.
Jamal	جمل	Camel. See H.Q. 7:40.
Jamrah	جمرة	Gravel of small pebbles, the three pillars in Minā at which the pilgrims throw pebbles after returning from 'Arafāt.
Jamrat-ul-'Aqabah	جمرة العقبه	The last pillar situated in Minā and a symbol of the Devil.
Janābah	جنابه	A state of uncleanliness after having a sexual discharge, either with your spouse or in a dream. A Muslim in such a state is not allowed to pray, recite Qurān or perform any kind of worship unless he performs Ghusl (a complete bath) or perform Tayam-mum, if applicable.
Janaf	جنف	Partially, wrong-doing, superstition. See H.Q. 2:182.
Janāzah	جنازه	Funeral service of a Muslim, a Muslim corpse.
Jan-nah Pl-Jan-nāt	جنة ـ جنات	Paradise, garden.
Jan-nātu 'Adn	جنات عدن	The Garden of Eden.

Jan-nat-ul-Khuld	جنة الخلد	The Garden of Eternity.
Jan-nat-ul-M'awā	جنة المأوى	The Gardens of Refute.
Jan-nāt-un-Na'īm	جنات النعيم	The Garden of Delight.
Jarād	جراد	Grasshoppers, locusts. See H.Q. 7:133.
al-Jāthiyah	الجاثية	"The Kneeling," the title of the 95th Sūra of the Holy Qurān.
al-Jawārī	الجواري	Plural of Jāriyah. Ships or any other sea vessels. See H.Q. 69:11
Jazā'	جزاء	Reward or punishment. See H.Q. 5:88.
Jaz'ah	جزعة	A five year old she-camel.
Jibrīl or Jibrā'īl	جبريل جبرائيل	The angel who brings down the revelations from Allāh (S.W.), to the prophets, Gabriel.
Jibt	جبت	Sorcery, divination, magic or any false object of belief to worship such as an idol. See H.Q. 4:51.
Jihād	جهاد	"An effort or strife." Holy fighting in the Cause of Allāh (S.W.) or any other kind of effort to make Allāh's word (al-Islām) superior. Jihād is regarded as one of the principles of al-Islām.
Jimālat-us-Ṣufr	جمالة صفر	Yellow camels, the yellow sparks flying swiftly one after another. See H.Q. 77:33.
Jimār	جمار	Plural of Jamrah.
Jinn	جن	An unseen creation of Allāh (S.W.); the Jinns were made from fire, as the human beings from mud and the angels from light.
Jin-nah	جنة	Madness, craziness, mental disturbance or the like. See H.Q. 7:148.
al-J'irānah	الجعرانة	A place a few miles away from Mecca. The Prophet (S.A.A.W.), distributed the war booty from the battle of Ḥunain there, and assumed the state of 'Iḥrām to perform 'Umra.

Jith'	جذع	The trunk of a tree. See H.Q. 19:33.
Jizyah	جزية	Head tax imposed by al-Islām on the non-Muslims who live under the rule of Dār-ul-'Islām. See H.Q 9:29.
Jub-b	جبّ	Well, a well of water. See H.Q. 12:10.
Jub-bah	جبة	A cloak or outer garment.
al-Juḥfah	الجحفة	The Miqāt of the people of Shām. The place where they declare the state of 'Ihrām. Also see Miqāt and Shām or Ash-Shām.
Jumād-al-'Ūlā	جمادى الاولى	The fifth month of the Muslim calendar.
Jumād-ath-Thāniyah or Ākhirah	جمادى الثانية	The sixth month of the Muslim calendar.
Jum'ah	جمعة	Friday.
Junub	جُنُب	One who is in the state of Janābah.
Junāḥ	جناح	Sin, a slight mistake. See H.Q. 2:158.
Jurhum	جرهم	The name of an Arab tribe from which 'Ismā'īl (A.A.), came.
Juz'	جز	One of the thirty (30) parts of the Holy Qurān.

—K—

Ka'bah	كعبة	The Cube. A cube-like building built by 'Ibrāhīm (A.A.) and 'Ismā'īl (A.A.), in the Center of the great Mosque in Mecca towards which all Muslims turn their face in prayer.
al-Kabīr	الكبير	"The Great One," one of the ninty-nine attributes of Allāh (S.W.).
Kafālah	كفالة	Bail, pledge, parole.
Kafara	كفر	Disbelieved.
Kaf-fārah	كفّارة	"To Hide." Coverings, expiation, atonements.
al-Kāfī	الكافي	"The Sufficient One," one of the ninty-nine attributes of Allāh (S.W.).

Kāfir Pl-Kuf-fār or Kāfirūn	كافر كفّار كافرون	Coverer. One who covers or hides truth, an infidel, non-believer, a disbeliever of Allāh (S.W.).
al-Kahf	الكهف	"The Cave," the title of the 18th Sūra of the Holy Qurān.
Kāhin	كاهن	Soothsayer, augur. See H.Q. 52:29.
Kahl	كهل	An old, aged person. See H.Q. 3:46.
Kaid	كيد	Plotting and planning against someone. See H.Q. 12:5.
Kail	كيل	Weighting, measuring. See H.Q. 12:59.
Kalām-ul-lāh	كلام الله	The words of Allāh (S.W.), The Holy Qurān.
Kalimah	كلمة	"Word," the creed of the Muslim, meaning: "None has the right to be worshipped but Allāh (S.W.), and Muḥammad (S.A.A.W.) is His Apostle."
Kalima-tush-Shahādah	كلمة الشهادة	"The word of testimony," a new Muslim has to confess that there is none to be worshipped but Allāh (S.W.), and Muḥammad (S.A.A.W.) is His Apostle and that he bears witness to that fact.
Kalīm-ul-lāh	كليم الله	"The Conversor with Allāh (S.W.)," the title of Prophet Moses (A.A.).
Kanīsah	كنيسه	A Christian church.
Kanīs	كنيس	A Jewish Synagogue.
Kanz	كنز	Treasure.
Karam	كرم	Generosity, hospitality.
al-Karīm	الكريم	"The Generous One," one of the ninty-nine attributes of Allāh (S.W.).
Kar-rah	كرّة	One more chance. See H.Q. 2:167.
Kashf	كشف	The uncovering of a secret, manifestation.
Katām	كتام	A plant used for dyeing hair.
Kithib	كذب	False, lying.

Kauthar كوثر See: al-Kauthar.

K͟habīth خبيث Wicked, base, impure.

K͟haḍirah خضرة A kind of vegatation, greenish color which indicates the presence of life, attraction.

K͟hafī خفي Hidden.

K͟haibar خيبر A well-known town which is rich and populous, located about eight stages (200 miles) north of al-Medīna.

K͟hairāt خيرات Plural of K͟hair. Good deeds, charity.

K͟halīfah خليفة "To leave behind." A caliph, successor, viceroy, deputy.

K͟halīl خليل This is superior to friend or beloved and is one of those whose love is mixed with one's soul. The Prophet had only one K͟halīl in Allāh (S.W.), but many friends, that K͟halīl was 'Abū Bakr (R.A.A.).

K͟halīlu-llāh خليل الله "The Friend of Allāh," a title given to Prophet 'Ibrāhīm (A.A.).

K͟halūf خلوف The changing in the smell of a fasting person.

K͟halūq خلوق A kind of perfume.

K͟hamr خمر Wine or any other alcoholic beverage or material which causes intoxication.

K͟hamaṣ خمص A severe hunger.

K͟hamīṣah خميصة A black woolen square blanket with marks on it.

al-K͟handaq الخندق The name of the battle between the Muslims and the infidels in al-Medīna, where a ditch was dug to defend the city.

al-K͟han-nās الخناس A demon, returning back.

K͟hanzab خنزب A demon causing doubt at the time of prayers.

K͟harāj خراج Taxes imposed on the yield of the land.

K͟hasafa خسف Eclipsed, used for a lunar eclipse. K͟hasafa al-Qamaru, the moon eclipsed.

Khashyah	خشية	Fear of Allāh (S.W.).
Khātam-un-Nabiyyīn	خاتم النبيين	"The Seal of the Prophets," meaning that he is the last of the prophets, Prophet Muḥammad bin 'Abdil-lāh (S.A.A.W.).
Khatam-un-Nubuwah	ختم النبوة	The Seal of the Prophecy, which some of the companions of the Prophet (S.A.A.W.) saw on back as a divine sign of his prophetic office.
Khāṭir	خاطر	Conscience, mind, memory.
Khatna	ختن	Circumcision.
Khauf	خوف	Fear of Allāh (S.W.).
Khazīrah	خزيرة	A special type of dish prepared from barley flour and meat soup which is cooked with water or milk and then eaten with dates. It is known also as Sakhīnah.
Khazraj	خزرج	A tribe settled in al-Medīna who embraced al-Islām in the early days.
Khil'ah	خلعة	A dress of honor presented by a ruler to an inferior, a mark of honor or distinction.
Khishāsh	خشاش	The creeping things of the earth.
Khishkhāsh	خشخاش	A kind of wild herb which grows naturally in the desert, used as a sedative or a calmant.
Khiyānah	خيانة	Breach of trust, betrayal.
Khuff	خفّ	Leather socks.
Khul'a	خلع	A kind of divorce in which the wife gives her husband a certain amount of compensation.
al-Khulafā'-ur-Rāshidūn	الخلفاء الراشدون	"The Well-Directed Caliphs," a title given to the first four caliphs of al-Islām, i.e. 'Abū Bakr, 'Umār, 'Uthmān and 'Alī.
Khumrah	خمرة	A small mat sufficient for the face and the hands used in prostation.
Khums	خمس	One fifth (⅕) of the war booty given to the Bait-ul-Māl, or public treasury. See H.Q. 8:41.
Khusūf	خسوف	Eclipse of the Moon. See Khasafa.

Khuṭbah خطبة The sermon or oration delivered on Friday before the prayer or at 'Īd prayers after the prayer and other occasions. Engagement, betrothal.

Khuṭba-tun-Nikāḥ خطبة النكاح A sermon delivered at the time of concluding a marriage ceremony.

Khuzaimah خزيمة A tribe expelled from the Yemen and settled in Ḥijāz (Saūdī Arabia).

Kibr كبر كِبْر Haughtiness, pride.

Karāmah كرامة The miracles of any saint other than a prophet.

Kirām-un-Kātibūn كرام كاتبون "Illustrious Writers." The recording angels, one on the left shoulder and the other on the right shoulder of each person, who write that person's good and bad deeds.

Kisrā كسرىٰ The King of Persia, Chosroes (Cyrus), Khusrau.

Kiswah كسوة A robe, the covering of the Holy Ka'ba in Mecca which has embroidered verses of the Holy Qurān.

al-Kitāb الكتاب "The Book," a term used for the Holy Qurān.

al-Kitāb-ul-Mubīn الكتاب المبين Tablet of Decrees, the Holy Qurān.

Kufr كفر Disbelief, infidelity, blasphemy. Also, the refusal of anything that the Prophet (S.A.A.W.) brought.

Kuḥl كحل Antimony Sulphide, an eye powder.

Kunyah كنية Agnomen. An Arabic and Islāmic custom consisting of "Abū" or "Umm" followed by the name of the son. For example, calling a man Abū 'Aḥmad (the father of 'Aḥmad) or calling a woman Umm 'Aḥmad (the mother of 'Aḥmad).

Kursī كرسي Chair. When used in regard to Āyat-al-Kursī, it means: "The Throne." See H.Q. 2:255.

Kusūf كسوف Eclipse of the sun.

—L—

Labbaik لبّيك Talbiyah, I respond to your call.

Labbaika-w Sa'daika	لَبَّيْك وسعديك	I respond to your call and I am obedient to your orders.
Lahd	لحد	The hollow made in a grave in the Qiblah side in which the corpse is placed.
Lahn	لحن	Speaking ungramatical 'Arabic, a certain way of speaking the language. See H.Q. 47:30.
Lailat-ul-Barā'ah	ليلة البراءة	The night of forgiveness.
al-Lailat-ul-Mubārakah	الليلة المباركة	The Blessed Night, Lailat-ul-Qadr. It is reported to be one of the odd numbered nights of the last ten nights of the month of Ramaḍān.
Lailat-ul-Qadr	ليلة القدر	The Night of Power. A mysterious and blessed night during the month of Ramaḍān.
Lailat-ur-ragh̲ā'ib	ليلة الرغائب	"The Night of Superogatory Devotion," the first Friday in the month of Rajab; said to have been established by the Prophet (S.A.A.W.) himself.
Lā-'Ilāha-'Ill-Allāh	لآإلٰه إلا الله	None has the right to be worshipped but Allāh (S.W.). The first pillar of declaring the Faith in al-Islām. The word of "at-Tawḥīd," the monotheism in al-Islām.
Layān	ليان	A kind of date.
Lamaza	لمز	Speaking ill, finding fault, to criticize, blame, backbite, slander, defame. See H.Q. 49:11.
Laqab	لقب	A title of honor, a nickname, a surname.
al-Lāt	اللات	An idol worshipped by Arab pagans.
Latḥā	لظى	A section of Hell mentioned in the Holy Qurān.
al-Laṭīf	اللطيف	"The Mysterious or the Subtle One," one of the ninty-nine attributes of Allāh (S.W.).
al-Lauḥ-ul-Maḥfūṭh	اللوح المحفوظ	"the Preserved Tablet" the tablet on which Allāh's decrees are written for all mankind.
Laun	لون	A kind of date.
Li'ān	لعان	"Mutual cursing." an oath which is taken by both the wife and the husband when he accuses his wife

		of committing adultery See H.Q. 24:6-9. Sūra Nūr.
Libās	لباس	Dress, apparel, garment.
Libās-ut-taqwā	لباس التقوىٰ	Decency, modesty in dressing. See H.Q. 7:26.
Liḥyah	لحية	Beard.
Limās	لماس	A sale in which the deal is completed when the buyer touches an item without seeing or checking it properly.
al-Lizām	اللزام	The settlement of affairs. In Ḥadīth, it refers to the battle of Badr which was the means of settling affairs between the Muslims and the pagans.
Lubb	لُبّ	The heart and soul of man.
al-Ludd	اللد	A small town in Palestine where it is said that Jesus (A.A.) will find al-Masīḥ-ad-Dajjāl and kill him.
Lughūb	لُغُوب	Exhaustion, lassitude, fatigue, great pain. See H. Q. 35:35.
Luj-jah	لُجَّة	Clamer, din, noise, hubbub. See H.Q. 27:44.
Lumazah	لُمَزَة	Fault finder, captious, critic. See H.Q. 104:1.
Luqṭah	لقطة	An article, property or anything found by someone other than the owner who has lost it, and preserved in trust.
Lūṭ	لوط	A Prophet of Allāh, whose followers were destroyed because they disobeyed the laws of Allāh. See H.Q. 11:70. Sūra Hūd.

—M—

Ma'āqil	معَاقل	Fines for manslaughter or murder.
al-Ma'ārij	المعَارج	"The Accents," the title of the 70th Sūra of the Holy Qurān.
Mabrak	مَبْرَك	The place of the camels' kneeling down.
Mubārak	مُبَارَك	Plural of Mabrak. Ṣalāt (prayer) is not permitted in those places as reported from Prophet Muhammad (S.A.A.W.).

Mabrūk	مبروك	Blessed. See Mubārik
Mabrūr	مبرور	Ḥajj accepted by Allāh (S.W.), for being perfectly performed.
Mafqūd	مفقود	A lost person, for whom information is obtainable.
Maghāfir	مغافر	A nasty smelling gum.
Maghḍūb	مغضوب	One who deserves the wrath. See H.Q. 1:7.
Maghrib	مغرب	The sunset, evening prayer.
al-Maḥaṣṣab	المحصب	A valley outside Mecca sometimes called Khaif Banī Kinānah, a tribe.
al-Mahdī	المهدي	"The Directed One." Guide, leader, one fit to guide others.
Maḥmal	محمل	A covered litter born or carried on a camel, a sign of royalty.
Mahr	مهر	Bridal money, dowry, money given by the husband to the wife upon marrying.
Maḥram	مَحْرَم	See Thū Maḥram.
al-Mā'idah	المائدة	"The Table," the title of the 5th Sūra of the Holy Qurān.
al-Maisir	المَيْسر	A game of chance. Forbidden in the Holy Qurān.
al-Majīd	المجيد	"The Glorious One," one of the ninty-nine attributes of Allāh (S.W.).
al-Majūs	المجوس	The Magians, a sect of eastern philosophers.
Makrūh	مكروه	That which is hateful and unbecoming. Not approved, undersirable from a religious point of view, although not punishable.
al-Malā'ikah	الملائكة	"The Angels," the title of the 35th Sūra of the Holy Qurān, the other title of this Sūra is "Fāṭir" or "The Creator."
al-Malik	الملك	"The Possessor, the Ruler, the Lord," one of the ninty-nine attributes of Allāh (S.W.). .
Mālik-ul-Mulk	مالك الملك	"The Lord of the Kingdom," one of the ninty-nine attributes of Allāh (S.W.).

Mamāt	ممات	Death.
Mamlūk	مملوك	A male slave.
Manārah	منارة	A minaret, pillar.
al-Manāsī	المناسي	A vast plateau on the outskirts of al-Medīna.
Manāsik	مناسك	The ceremonies of Ḥajj. These include all of the rites required for performing a correct Ḥajj.'
Manāt	مناة	An idol mentioned in the Holy Qurän of the tribes of the Ḥuthail.
al-Māni'	المانع	"The Witholder," one of the ninty-nine attributes of Allāh (S.W.).
Maniḥah **Pl-Manā'ih**	منيحة مناتح	A certain sort of gift in the form of a she-camel or sheep given to someone temporarily so that its milk may be used and then the animal is returned to the owner later.
al-Mann	المنّ	A food supplied by Allāh (S.W.), to the Children of 'Isrāel. See H.Q. 2:57.
Mansik	منسك	Place of sacrifice, ceremony, ritual during pilgrimage.
Maqām **'Ibrāhīm**	مقام ابراهيم	The position where Prophet 'Ibrāhīm (A.A.) stood while he and 'Ismā'īl were building the Ka'ba in Mecca.
Maqām-un- **Maḥmūd**	مقام محمود	"A Glorious Station." The highest place in Paradise reserved for Prophet Muhammad (S.A.A.W.) only and none else.
Marās	مراس	A place nearer to Minā than Ash-shajara.
Marthiyyah	مرثيّة	A funeral elegy in poetic form.
al-Marwah	المروة	A hill near the Ka'ba, the end point of Sa'ī.
Masḥ	مسح	The act of touching the head or socks for purification during ablution with fingers wetted with water.
al-Masīḥ	المسيح	Surname of Jesus (A.A.).
al-Masīḥ-ad- **Dajjāl**	المسيح الدّجّال	"The Lying Jesus," the anti-Jesus which Prophet Muḥammad (S.A.A.W.) predicted will appear before the day of Resurrection.

al-Masjid-al-'Aqṣā	المسجد الأقصى	"The most distant Mosque." The temple at Jerusalem erected by Prophet Solomon (A.A.), also known as "Baitul-Maqdis" or Umar's Mosque.
al-Masjid-ul-Ḥarām	المسجد الحرام	The Great Mosque in Mecca in which the Ka'ba is located. "Bait-ullāh" denotes the whole structure.
Masjid-ul-Khaif	مسجد الخيف	The mosque in Minā, three (3) miles from Mecca.
Masjid-un-Nabī	مسجد النبى	"The Prophet's Mosque" at al-Medīna the second most important Mosque in the world of al-Islām.
Masjid-ut-Taqwā	مسجد التقوى	The mosque at Qubā'. The first mosque built in al-Medīna. It is located at a place about three (3) miles southeast of the city where Prophet Muḥammad's she-camel, al-Qaṣwā', rested on its way from Mecca on the occasion of his Hijrah.
Masnūn	مسنون	Founded on the traditions of Prophet Muḥammad (S.A.A.W.).
al-Mathānī	المثاني	Sūras of the Holy Qurān. Prophet Muḥammad (S.A.A.W.) says that Sab'a al-Mathānī is Sūra al-Fātiḥah.
al-Matīn	المتين	"The Strong," one of the ninty-nine attributes of Allāh (S.W.).
Maulā	مولى	Manumitted slave, Master or Lord. Also used for a freed slave.
Maulāī	مولاي	My Lord, My Master. An expression used when a slave addresses his master.
Maulid	مولد	Birthday. The birthday of the Prophet (S.A.A.W.), Maulid-un-Nabī, is celebrated on the 12th of Rabī'-ul-'Awwal.
Mā'ūn	ماعون	A little help, a small kindness. See H.Q. 107:7.
Maut	موت	Death, departure of the spirit from the body.
Miftāḥ-ul-Jannah	مفتاح الجنّة	"The Key of Paradise." A term used by Prophet Muḥammad (S.A.A.W.), for prayer.
Miḥjan	مِحْجَن	A hook-headed stick about four (4) feet long carried by the Prophet (S.A.A.W.), which is now carried by some religious men.

Miḥrāb	محراب	A niche in the center of a front wall of a Mosque denoting the direction of the Qiblah; also, used by the Imām to lead prayer.
Mijannah	مجنّة	A place at Mecca.
Mikhḍab	مخضب	A painted stone pot.
Millah	ملّة	The religion of Prophet 'Ibrāhīm (A.A.), al-Islām. A path, way, creed, faith.
Minā	منىٰ	"A Wish." A valley outside Mecca on the way to 'Arafāt. It is five (5) miles away from Mecca and about ten (10) miles from 'Arafāt.
Minbar	منبر	The pulpit in a mosque from where the Khuṭba is delivered.
Mīqāt	ميقات	"A Stated Time or Place." The places from which the Pilgrims to Mecca assume the state of 'Iḥrām.
Mi'raj	معراج	"An Ascent." Prophet Muḥammad's journey to the Seven Heavens.
Mirbad	مربد	A place where dates are dried.
Miskīn	مسكين	A poor person.
Miṣr	مصر	Egypt, a country without defining a name.
Miswāk	مسواك	A teeth cleaner made from a branch of a tree called 'Arāk.
Mithqāl	مثقال	A gram and three sevenths. Also used for a gold coin of that weight.
Mīzān	ميزان	Balance, scales.
Muḥkam	محكم	Qur'ānic verses which are not abrogated. Those verses which are irrevocable.
Mu'ath-thin	مؤذّن	A Muslim man who pronounces the 'Āthān loudly calling the people to come and perform the prayers.
al-Mu'akh-khir	المؤخّر	"The Deferrer," one of the ninty-nine attributes of Allāh (S.W.).
Mu'ānaqah	معانقة	Embracing, neck to neck, kissing.
al-Mu'aqqibāt	المعقّبات	The title of the writing angel, Kirām-un-Kātibūn.

al-Mu'aw-wathtān	المعوّذتان	Sūrat-al-Falaq (#113) and Sūrat-an-Nas (#114) of the Holy Qurān.
Mubāḥ	مباح	Permitted, allowed.
Mubārak	مُبارَك	Blessed. See Mabrūk.
Mubārakah	مُباركه	To offer blessings or to seek Allāh's blessings for someone.
Mubārāt	مباراة	Mutual discharge. see Khal'.
al-Mubdī'	المبدئ	"The beginner or Producter," one of the ninty-nine attributes of Allāh (S.W.).
Mūbiqāt	موبقات	Great destructive sins.
Mudabbar	مدبّر	A slave who is promised to be freed or manumitted after his/her master's death.
Mudd	مدّ	A measure equal to two thirds (⅔) of a kilogram.
Mudda'i	مدّع	The plaintiff in a lawsuit, complainant.
Mudda'ā 'Alaih	مدّعىعليه	The defendant in a lawsuit.
al-Mud-dath-thir	المدّثر	"The Wrapped One," the title of the 74th Sūra of the Holy Qurān.
Mufsid	مفسد	A pernicious person.
Muftī	مفتي	A learned Islāmic leader who gives or is qualified to give legal Islāmic verdicts.
Mufaṣ-ṣal or Mufaṣ-ṣalah	مفصّل مفصّلة	The Sūras from Sūrat-Qāf to the end of the Holy Qurān.
al-Mughnī	المغني	"The Enricher," one of the ninty-nine attributes of Allāh (S.W.).
Muḥad-dith	محدّث	A narrator of Ḥadīth, a learned man in Ḥadīth.
al-Muhaimin	المهيمن	"The Protector," one of the ninty-nine attributes of Allāh (S.W.).
Muhājir **Pl-Muhājirūn**	مهاجر مهاجرون	Any of the early Muslims who had emigrated to al-Medīna in the lifetime of Prophet Muḥammad (S.A.A.W.), before the conquest of Mecca. One

who quits all things forbidden by Allāh (S.W:). One who leaves a country ruled by an infidel or unbeliever leader.

Muḥal-lil محلّل One who marries a divorced wife in order that her former husband can marry her again after obtaining a divorce from the Muḥal-lil. A Muḥal-lil is one who has been cursed by Prophet Muḥammad (S.A.A.W.). This action is hated by the Prophet (S.A.A.W.).

Muḥāqalah محاقلة The sale of wheat still in ears for pure wheat.

Muḥarram محرّم The first month of the Muslim calendar. Forbidden.

Muḥrim مُحْرِم
Fem-Muḥrimah مُحْرِمَة One who assumes the state of 'Iḥrām for performing Ḥajj or 'Umra.

Muḥsan مُحْصَن
Fem-Muḥṣanah مُحْصَنَة Caused to be content or chaste, to be abstained from that which is unlawful or indecorous by his wife. A married man. See H.Q. 4:24.

Muḥṣar مُحْصَر A Muḥrim who intends to perform Ḥajj or 'Umra but cannot do so as a result of some obstacle.

al-Muḥṣī المحصي "The Counter," one of the ninty-nine attributes of Allāh (S.W.).

Muḥtasib محتسب An oppointed official by a ruler to enforce the Islāmic laws and to punish those who violate them.

al-Muḥyī المحيي "The Life Giver," one of the ninty-nine attributes of Allāh (S.W.).

al-Mu'īd المعيد "The Restorer," one of the ninty-nine attributes of Allāh (S.W.).

al-Mu'izz المعزّ "The Giver of Honor," one of the ninty-nine attributes of Allāh (S.W.).

Mujāhid مجاهد
Pl-Mujāhidūn مجاهدون A warrier in the Cause of Allāh (S.W.).

Mujaz-zah مجزّة The name of the land in which the false Messiah will appear.

al-Mujīb المجيب "The Respondent," one of the ninty-nine attributes of Allāh (S.W.).

Mu'jizah	معجزة	A miracle given to the Prophets of Allāh (S.W.). For example, the revelation of the H.Q. to Prophet Muḥammad (S.A.A.W.), the splitting of the Red Sea by Prophet Moses (A.A.) and the healing of the sick by Prophet Jesus (A.A.).
Mujtahid	مجتهد	One who is trying to gain knowledge and learning. One who contributes to Islāmic jurisprudence in various affairs.
Mukātab	مُكَاتَب	A slave, male or female, who binds himself/herself to pay a certain ransom or fee for freedom.
Mukhābarah	مخابرة	The sale of grain, free from disease and blights, before it is ripe - its benefit is evident.
Mukhaddarah	مخدّرة	A woman in a state of purity, a veiled woman.
Mukhālaṭah	مخالطة	Intermixing. Sexual intercourse between two unclean persons.
Mulā'anah	ملاعنة	The act of performing Li'ān. See Li'ān.
Mulḥid	ملحد	An infidel, a disbeliever.
al-Mulk	المُلك	"The Kingdom," the title of the 67th Sūra of the Holy Qurān.
Mu'min	مؤمن	A believer. The title of the 40th Sūra of the Holy Qurān.
al-Mu'minūn	المومنون	"The Believers," the title of the 23rd Sūra of the Holy Qurān.
al-Mumīt	المميت	"The Killer," one of the ninty-nine attributes of Allāh (S.W.).
Mumsik	ممسك	A miserly person.
al-Mumtaḥinah	الممتحنة	"One who is Tried," the title of the 60th Sūra of the Holy Qurān.
Munābathah	منابذة	A synonym of Nibāth. See Nibāth.
Munāfiq	منافق	A hyprocrite, one who says one thing and does the opposite.
al-Munāfiqūn	المنافقون	"The Hyprocrites," the title of the 63rd Sūra of the Holy Qurān.

Munājāh	مناجاة	Whispering to, confidential talk. The private prayers or invocations to Allāh (S.W.), offered after performing the Farḍ prayers.
Munaṣṣaf	منصّف	A forbidden alcoholic drink made by evaporating fermented grapes to one half (½) of its original volume.
Munfiq	منفق.	One who spends in the name of Allāh (S.W.).
Munkar-a-Nakīr	منكر ونكير	The two angels who will come into the graves of every person to take account of his good and bad deeds of this world.
al-Muntaqim	المنتقم	"The Avenger," one of the ninty-nine attributes of Allāh (S.W.).
al-Muqaddim	المقدّم	"The Forward Bringer," one of the ninty-nine attributes of Allāh (S.W.).
Muqaiyar	المقير	The name of the type of pot in which alcoholic drinks are prepared.
Muqāyaḍah	مقايضة	Giving in equal value, barter. For example, exchanging 10 eggs for a pound of dates.
al-Muqīt	المقيت	"The Mighty or Guardian," one of tḥe ninty-nine attributes of Allāh (S.W.).
al-Muqsiṭ	المقسط	"The Equitable," one of the ninty-nine attributes of Allāh (S.W.).
Muqtadin	مقتدٍ	A follower, a person praying behind an 'Imām in a prayer.
al-Muqtadir	المقتدر	"The Prevailing or Powerful," one of the ninty-nine attributes of Allāh (S.W.).
Murābaḥah	مرابحة	Selling for profit disclosing the cost of the purchase at the same time.
Murāhanah	مراهنة	Bet, wager. This act is Ḥarām in al-Islām; however, it is permitted in terms of lien.
Murāhaqah	مراهقة	Arriving in Mecca when Ḥajj ceremonies are almost over. Also, puberty or adolescence.
Murāqabah	مراقبة	Contemplation, meditation, devotion.

Mursal	مُرسَل	A Messenger or an Apostle who brings a book or holy scripture from Allāh (S.W.). Also, a type of Ḥadīth in which a main Ṣaḥābī is missing in the chain of narrators.
al-Mursalāt	المرسلات	"The Sent People," the title of the 77th Sūra of the Holy Qurān.
Murshid	مرشد	A guide, a spiritual leader.
Murtadd	مرتدّ	One who has rejected al-Islām. In al-Islām or in the Islāmic laws, beheading is the punishment for such a person.
Muṣāfaḥah	مصافحة	Shaking hands, common among Muslims all over the world. However, according to the Sunnah of the Prophet (S.A.A.W.), men should not shake the hands of women.
Muṣal-lā	مصلّى	A small mat, prayer rug or carpet, a praying place.
al-Muṣaw-wir	المصوّر	"The Painter," one of the ninty-nine attributes of Allāh (S.W.).
Mushrik **Pl-Mushrikūn**	مشرك مشركون	Those who associate others with Allāh (S.W.).
Muslim	مسلم	One who completely submits to the Will of Allāh (S.W.).
Mustaḥāḍah	مستحاضة	A woman who has vaginal bleeding between her periods. In this case, she should perform Ghusl and then pray.
Mut'ah	مُتعَة	A temporary marriage contract when one was away from his home for a long period of time. This specific type of marriage contract was allowed in the early periods of al-Islām; but later, it was cancelled and forbidden, and is Ḥarām.
al-Muta'āl	المتعال	"The Exalted," one of the ninty-nine attributes of Allāh (S.W.).
Mutafaḥ-ḥish	متفحّش	A person who conveys evil talk.
al-Mutakab-bir	المتكبر	"The Proud, the Great," one of the ninty-nine attributes of Allāh (S.W.).
Mu'takif	معتكف	One who is in the state of 'I'tikāf. See 'I'tikāf.

Mu'tamir معتمر One who performs 'Umra.

Mutashābihāt متشابهات The Qur'ānic Verses or Āyāt which are hard to understand or allegorical.

Mutawal-li متول A person responsible for the running of the various kinds of activities of a religious place, such as: administration, finance and the like.

al-Muthil-l المذل "The Abaser," one of the ninty-nine attributes of Allāh (S.W.).

al-Mu'ṭī المعطي "The Giver," one of the ninty-nine attributes of Allāh (S.W.).

Mu'tiq معتق One who manumits or frees a slave.

Mut-taqīn متّقين God-fearing or pious people.

Muwaḥ-ḥid موّحد One who believes in one God (Allāh).

Muzābanah مزابنة The sale of fresh dates or fresh grapes for dry dates or grapes by measure. The dried fruits are measured while the fresh ones are only estimated as they are still uncut.

Muzaffāt مزفاة The name of the pot in which alcoholic drinks are prepared.

al-Muzdalifah المزدلفة A place or a valley between Minā and 'Arafāt where the pilgrams returning from 'Arafāt spend a night between the ninth (9th) and tenth (10th) of Thul-Ḥijjah. Pebbles are collected here to be thrown at Jamrāt.

al-Muzammil المزمّل "The Wrapped One," the title of the 74th Sūra of the Holy Qurān. Prophet Muḥammad (S.A.A.W.) was "The Wrapped One", implied by this title.

—N—

an-Nabā' النبأ "The Information, the News;" the title of the 78th Sūra of the Holy Qurān.

Nabī نبي One who receives inspiration through an angel of Allāh (S.W.).

Nabīth نبيذ Water in which dates and grapes are soaked which is not yet fermented and lawful to drink.

Nadā	ندى	Generosity. Also, dew.
Nadam	ندم	Repentance, regretting.
Naḍīḥah	نضيحة	A camel used for agricultural purposes.
an-Nāfi'	النافع	"The Profiter," one of the ninty-nine attributes of Allāh (S.W.).
Nafkha	نفخ	Blasting of the bugle on the Day of Resurrection by 'Isrāfīl, the angel assigned for this job.
Nafl or Nāfilah Pi, Nawāfil	نفل نافلة نوافل	A voluntary act. Optional practice of worship.
Nafqah	نفقة	The alimony or the maintenance of the wife and children as a settlement of a divorce.
Nafr	نفر	The 12th day of the month of Thul-Ḥijjah when the pilgrims leave Minā after performing all of the ceremonies of Ḥajj at 'Arafāt, Muzdalifah and Minā.
Nafs	نفس	Soul, human desires, animal life, conscience.
Nafsā'	نفساء	A woman in a state of Nifās, bleeding after childbirth. The "confinement."
an-Naḥl	النحل	"The Bees," the title of the 16th Sūra of the Holy Qurān.
an-Najaf	النجف	A town in central 'Irāq.
Najd	نجد	The desert of Saūdī 'Arabia, the 'Arabian Highland.
Najl	نجل	Son, offspring.
Najrān	نجران	A region between Saūdī 'Arabia and the Yemen.
Naḥr	نحر	The slaughtering of the camels only by cutting the carotid artery located at the root of the neck. The day of Naḥr is the 10th day of the month of Thul-Ḥijja on which all Pilgrims slaughter their sacrifice.
Nā'ib	نائب	Khalīfah, deputy, lieutenant.
Najas or Najāsah	نجس نجاسة	Impurity,uncleanliness.Impurity of any kind.

Najash نجش Offering a high price for something without having the intention to buy it just to cheat someone else who really wants to buy the item. Such a person may agree with the seller to offer high prices in an auction to boost the prices. In this case, the Najash and the seller are sinful.

an-Najm النجم "The Star," the title of the 53rd Sūra of the Holy Qurān.

Najwā نجوى Confidential talk between Allāh (S.W.) and His devotees on the Day of Judgement. It is a favor from Allāh (S.W.) to the devotees or the believers. Any confidential talk between Allāh (S.W.) and His devotees.

Nakhlah نخلة A valley between Mecca and Ṭā'if. The scene of the first fight between the Muslims and the 'Arab Pagans.

Nākiḥ ناكح A married man. Mankūḥah - a married woman.

Namīmah نميمة Calumnies. The conveyance of disagreeable or false information from one person to another to create hostility between them.

an-Naml النمل "The Ants," the title of the 27th Sūra of the Holy Qurān.

Nāmūs ناموس The angel who appeared to Moses (A.A.), according to Waraqah.

Naqīb نقيب Tribal chief. A person heading a group of 6 (six) persons.

Naqīr نقير The name of the pot in which alcoholic drinks are prepared.

an-Nār النار "The Fire." Commonly used as a name for Hell or the Hell-Fire.

an-Nās الناس "The Mankind," the title of the last or the 114th Sūra of the Holy Qurān.

Nasab نسب Lineage, family, race, kinship.

Naṣārā نصارى The followers of the Christian faith.

Nasī'ah نسيئة Credit, delay of payment.

Nāsik	ناسك	A pious person, a devotee.
Nāsikh	ناسخ	A verse of the Qurān which cancels or abrogates a previous one.
Naskh	نسخ	Cancellation.
Nasr	نسر	One of the old Arabian pagan idols mentioned in the Holy Qurān.
an-Naṣr	النّصر	"Help," the title of the 110th Sūra of the Holy Qurān.
Naṣṣ	نصّ	A demonstration. An express or well-defined law of the Holy Qurān or Ḥadīth.
Naṣṣ-un-Karīm	نصّ كريم	"The Gracious Revelation," The Holy Qurān.
Naṣūḥ	نصوح	Sincerity in repentance to Allāh (S.W.). Friendship.
Nathara	نَذَرَ	To dedicate, to vow to Allāh (S.W.), to make a solemn pledge.
Nathr	نَذر	Vow, solemn pledge.
Nawḥ	نوح	Lamentations for the dead. It is forbidden in al-Islām to hire someone for this purpose.
Nawā'ib	نوائب	Disasters, calamities, misfortunes.
an-Nāzi'āt	النازعات	"Those Who Tear Out," the title of the 79th Sūra of the Holy Qurān.
Nazaha	نزه	To be free, to steer clear.
Nazgh	نزغ	Incitement of evil, Satanic inspiration.
Nazr	نَزر	Insignificant, little, negligible, portion.
Nibāz	نِبَاز	A sale in which the deal is completed when a seller throws an item towards the buyer giving him no opportunity to see it or to check it.
Nifāq	نفاق	Hypocrisy, to say one thing and to act in the opposite manner.
Nifās	نفاس	The state of confinement of a woman after childbirth.

Nikāḥ	نكاح	A marriage contract or wedlock according to Islāmic law.
Nikẖāsah	نخاسة	Cattle trade, slave trade.
Nikẖāmah	نخامة	Phlegm, mucus, spitting out.
an-Nisā'	النساء	"The Women," the title of the 4th Sūra of the Holy Qurān.
Niṣāb	نصاب	Property or estate on which Zakāt must be paid at the rate of 2½% of its net value.
Niyyah	نيّة	Intention, purpose, vow.
Nubu-wwah	نبوّة	Prophecy. The office of a Prophet.
Nūn	نون	The letter "Nūn" in the Arabic alphabet. Fish.
an-Nuqabā'	النقباء	The chiefs or representative leaders. Plural of Naqīb. See Naqīb.
an-Nūr	النور	"The Light," one of the ninty-nine attributes of Allāh (S.W.). Also, the title of the 24th Sūra of the Holy Qurān.
an-Nūr-ul 'Anwar	النور الانور	"The Light of the Lights." Allāh (S.W.), the divine being.
Nusk	نُسْك	A religious ceremony.
Nusuk	نُسُك	A sacrifice.
Nuzūl	نزول	The revealing or the descent of the Holy Qurān in small portions from Allāh (S.W.) to Prophet Muḥammad (S.A.A.W.), through Angel Jibrīl (A.A.).

—Q—

Qabā'	قباء	An outer garment with full sleeves.
Qābala	قابل	To transfer the deed of a property, signed by a judge.
Qāba Qausain	قاب قوسين	Jibrīl (A.A.). Nearness to Allāh (S.W.).
al-Qābiḍ	القابض	"The Restrainer," one of the ninty-nine attributes of Allāh (S.W.).
Qabr	قبر	A grave, tomb.

Qabūl	قبول	The consent of both the bride and groom without which Nikāḥ is not valid.
Qa'dah	قعده	The sitting position in prayer during which Tashahhud is recited.
al-Qadīm	القديم	"The Ancient, the Old. Allāh (S.W.), The Everlasting.
al-Qādir	القادر	"The Powerful," one of the ninty-nine attributes of Allāh (S.W.).
al-Qadr	القَدْر	"Measuring," the title of the 97th Sūra of the Holy Qurān. Also "Power".
al-Qadr	القَدْر	One of the odd nights of the last 10 (ten) days of the month of Ramaḍān described by Allāh (S.W.), as better than one thousand months. One who worships Allāh (S.W.), during this night will get great rewards. See Lailat-ul-Qadr.
Qāf	قاف	A letter in the Arabic alphabet. The title of the 50th Sūra of the Holy Qurān.
al-Qah-hār	القهّار	"The Dominant," one of the ninty-nine attributes of Allāh (S.W.).
Qā'if	قائف	Learned in the act of knowing footsteps. A judge of character.
Qailūlah	قيلوله	A mid-day nap.
Qainuqā'	قينقاع	A jewish tribe near al-Medīna who were sent into exile by Prophet Muḥammad (S.A.A.W.), in the second year of Hijra.
Qaiṣar	قيصر	Julius Caesar of Rome.
al-Qaiy-yūm	القيّوم	"The Self-Subsisting," one of the ninty-nine attributes of Allāh (S.W.).
al-Qalam	القلم	"The Pen," the title of the 68th Sūra of the Holy Qurān.
Qalīb	قليب	A well ouside al-Medīna where almost 40 Ṣaḥābī who were Ḥāfiṭh of the Holy Qurān were killed in a trap.
al-Qamar	القمر	"The Moon," the title of the 54th Sūra of the Holy Qurān.

Qanā'ah	قناعة	Resignation, contentment, moderation.
Qarābah	قرابة	Relationship, nearness.
Qāniṭ	قانط	Standing in prayer before Allāh (S.W.). Godly, devout.
Qānit	قانت	Desparing, desparate. This state of mind is discouraged by Allāh (S.W.).
Qānūn	قانون	A law, a statute. A rule, a regulation.
Qārī' **Pl-Qur-rā'**	قارى قرّاء	A reciter of the Holy Qurān, a religious scholar, the teachers of early Muslims.
al-Qāri'ah	القارعة	"The Striking," the title of the 101st Sūra of the Holy Qurān.
Qārin	قارن	One who performs Ḥajj-al-Qirān.
Qarn-ul-Manāzil	قرن المنازل	The Mīqāt of the people of Najd. It is situated between Ṭā'if and Mecca.
Qaṣab	قصب	Pipes made of pearls and other precious stones.
Qasam	قسم	An oath, vow.
Qāsama	قاسم	Taking an oath or a vow that the accused did not kill.
al-Qaṣaṣ	القصص	"The Narrative," the title of the 28th Sūra of the Holy Qurān.
Qasm	قسم	Division of conjugal rights as permitted by Islāmic law. For example, when a person dies whose parents are still living and has brothers and sisters, his mother shoud inherit ⅙ (one-sixth) of the wealth of the deceased.
al-Qaṣwā'	القصواء	"One whose ears are cropped." The name of Prophet Muḥammad's she-camel on which he migrated to al-Medīna from Mecca.
Qaṯhf	قذف	Accusation of adultery. If false, the punishment is 80 lashes.
Qaṭīfah	قطيفة	A thick, soft cloth with a hairy surface.
Qatl	قتل	Murder, manslaughter.

attāt	قتّات	A slanderer. A person who conveys information from one person to another with the intention to cause harm and enmity between them.
Qaul	قول	A promise, a saying, a covenant.
Qaul-ul-Ḥaqq	قول الحقّ	"Word of Truth." A title given to Prophet Jesus (A.A.), in the Holy Qurān.
al-Qawwī	القوّى	"The Strong," one of the ninty-nine attributes of Allāh (S.W.).
Qiblah	قبلة	"Anything in front." The direction in which all Muslims must turn their faces in the prayers, i.e., towards the Ka'ba in Mecca.
Qimār	قمار	Gambling, dice, a game of chance. Forbidden by Islāmic law.
Qinn	قن	A slave born of slave parents.
Qinṭār	قنطار	A talent, a very large amount of money. Also, a varying weight of 100 lb. Ratl (in Eg. = 44.93kg. in Tunisia = 53.9kg, in Syria = 256.4kg).
Qirā'h	قراءة	Chanting of the Holy Qurān. Also see Tajwīd.
Qirām	قرام	A thin marked woolen curtain.
Qirān	قران	Ḥajj performed with 'Umra in the same state of 'Iḥrām. Hadī is to be brought along by the pilgrim and offered on the Day of Naḥr when performing this type of Ḥajj.
Qīrāṭ	قيراط	A large weight equal to ½ Dāniq. One (1) Dirham is equal to six (6) Dāniq.
Qiṣāṣ	قصاص	The law of equality in punishment, the law of retaliation.
Qissī	قسّي	A kind of cloth containing silk. It is named Qissī because it is largely manufactured in a city called Qis in Egypt.
Qithām	قذام	A disease which causes the fruits to fall off the trees before ripening.
Qiyāfah	قيافة	The science of tracing one's origin.

Qiyām	قيام	"Standing." In prayer and reciting all of the prescribed verses, Yaum-ul-Qiyāmah means the Day of Judgement.
al-Qiyāmah	القيامة	Standing up. The Day of Resurrection. The title of the 75th Sūra of the Holy Qurān.
Qiyās	قياس	To compare. The fourth (4th) foundation of Islāmic Jurisprudence in which logical reasoning is used by learned people in teaching al-Islām.
Qubā'	قباء	A place three (3) miles from al-Medīna where al-Qaṣwā', the she-camel of the Prophet (S.A.A.W.), stopped on the journey from Mecca. A mosque has been built there and bears the same name. According to the sayings of Prophet Muḥammad (S.A.A.W.), a visit to that particular mosque on a Saturday afternoon and offering a two (2) Rak'āt prayer is regarded equal to the performance of an 'Umra.
al-Qud-dūs	القدّوس	"The Sacred," one of the ninty-nine attributes of Allāh (S.W.).
Qudrah	قدرة	Power, Omnipotence.
Qum-Qum	قمقم	A narrow-headed vessel used for fragrance or blossom water.
Qunūt	قنوت	A special invocation offered in the Witr Prayer at night or after the second Rukū' in the Fajr prayer.
Quraiṭhah	قُرَيظَة	A Jewish tribe near al-Medīna which was completely destroyed by Prophet Muḥammad (S.A.A.W.), on the order of Allāh (S.W.) due to their betrayal.
Qurān	قرآن	The Holy Book revealed to Prophet Muḥammad (S.A.A.W.), from Allāh (S.W.), in parts through Angel Jibrīl (A.A.). The ever readable book.
Quraish	قريش	One of the greatest tribes in Arabia during the pre-Islāmic era, which had great powers spiritually and financially both before and after the advent of al-Islām. Prophet Muḥammad (S.A.A.W.), was born into this tribe.
Quraishī	قريشي	A person belonging to the tribe of Quraish. See Quraish.

Qurbān	قُربَان	An offering, a sacrifice.
Quṭb	قطب	An axis, a stake, a pivot. A knowledgeable person in al-Islām. This term is mainly used in Ṣūfism.

—R—

ar-Rabb	الرّب	"The Lord, the Owner," one of the ninty-nine attributes of Allāh (S.W.). The Provider.
Rab-buka	ربّك	Your Lord, your Master, Allāh (S.W.).
ar-Rabat͟hah	الرّبذة	A place in the desert of Saūdī Arabia about three (3) stages from al-Medīna.
Rabī'-ul-'Aw-wal	ربيع الأوّل	The third (3rd) month of the Muslim calendar
ar-Ra'd	الرّعد	"The Thunder," the title of the 13th Sūra of the Holy Qurān.
Radd	ردّ	Rejection, abrogation, repell, reply, refutation.
Radd-us-Salām	ردّ السّلام	Replying to a salutation. Obligatory to every Muslim.
ar-Rafī'	الرّفيع	"The Exalter," one of the ninty-nine attributes of Allāh (S.W.).
Rāhib	راهب	A Christian monk, a padre.
Rāḥil	راحل	Fit for traveling. Also, a folding book stand used for the Holy Qurān.
Rāḥilah	راحلة	A she-camel used for riding, a mount to ride.
ar-Raḥīm	الرحيم	"The Compassionate," one of the ninty-nine attributes of Allāh (S.W.).
Raḥmah	رحمة	Compassion, mercy.
ar-Raḥmān	الرّحمٰن	"The Merciful," one of the ninty-nine attributes of Allāh (S.W.).
Rahn	رهن	Pawning or pledging.
Rā'inā	راعنا	A word whose use is forbidden. See H.Q. 2:104.
Raiyyān	ريّان	"One whose thirst is quenched," the name of one of the gates of Paradise through which the

observers of the fasting during the month of Ramaḍān will enter.

Rajab رجب The seventh (7th) month of the Muslim calendar.

Raj'ah رجعة The continuance of the marriage bond before the divorce becomes valid.

Rajaz رجز The name of a poetic meter.

Rajīm رجيم "One who is stoned." The name given to Satan.

Rajm رجم Stoning to death as a penalty for adultery.

Rak'ah ركعة A section of the prayer. To bow, to prostrate.

Ramaḍān رمضان The ninth (9th) month of the Muslim calendar, the month of fasting. In this month, the Holy Qurān was revealed to Muḥammad (S.A.A.W.), and also, the decisive battle of Badr was won by the Muslims. See also Lailat-ul-Qadr.

Ramal رَمَل Fast walking accompanied by the movement of the arms and the legs to show one's body strength. This is to be observed by men only during the first three (3) rounds of the Ṭawāf around the Ka'ba because the Prophet (S.A.A.W.) practised it as such. Also, a poetic meter.

Ramī or Ramī-ul-Jimār رمي / رمي الجمار The throwing of pebbles at the Jimār in Minā during Ḥajj.

ar-Raqīb الرّقيب "The One Who Watches Over," one of the ninty-nine attributes of Allāh (S.W.).

ar-Rashīd الرّشيد "The Rightly Guided," one of the ninty-nine attributes of Allāh (S.W.).

Rasm رسم Custom, law. That which is stamped or sealed.

Rasūl رسول An apostle of Allāh (S.W.), who was given a book.

Ratl رَتْل Single file.

ar-Rauḍah الرّوضه The garden in which the tomb of Prophet Muḥammad (S.A.A.W.), is located.

ar-Ra'ūf الرّؤوف "The Kind," one of the ninty-nine attributes of Allāh (S.W.).

Rawdāt-ul-Khawkh	روضة الخوخ	A place between Mecca and al-Medīna.
ar-Raz-zāq	الرّزاق	"The Provider," one of the ninty-nine attributes of Allāh (S.W.).
Ribā	رِبَا	Usury, interest. There are two (2) kinds of Ribā both of which are strictly forbidden by the laws of al-Islām: (1) Ribā Nasī'ah - interest on lent money. (2) Ribā Faḍl - taking a superior thing of the same kind by giving more of the same kind of goods of an inferior quality. For example, giving dates of a superior quality for dates of an inferior quality in a larger amount.
Ribāṭ	رِبَاط	A fort in enemy territory constructed for Muslim soldiers.
Ridā'	رداء	A sheet that is worn around the upper part of the body.
Riḍwān	رضوان	The name of the gatekeeper or gardner in Paradise.
Rihān	رِهَان	Pawning or pledge. See Rahn.
Rikāz	رِكاز	Buried treasure or wealth form the pre-Islāmic period.
Risālah	رسالة	The office of an apostle or a prophet.
Riwāyah	رواية	A narration from another person, a Ḥadīth.
Riyā'	رِيَاء	Hyprocrisy, deceit, dissimulation, pretension.
Rub'	رُبع	One fourth (¼). The share of a wife in her husband's wealth if he dies issueless.
Rūḥ	رُوح	The spirit, the soul, the life.
Rūḥ-ullāh	رُوح الله	The Spirit of Allāh (S.W.). According to Prophet Muḥammad(S.A.A.W.), it is a special title for Jesus (A.A.).
ar-Rūḥ-ul-'Amīn	الرّوح الامين	"The Faithful Spirit," the Angel Jibrīl (A.A.).
Rūḥ-ul-Qudus	رُوح القدس	"The Holy Spirit," meaning Angel Jibrīl.

ar-Rukn-ul-Yamānī	الرّكن اليماني	The southern part of the Ka'ba facing Yemen. The stone embedded in the corner is supposed to be the most ancient part of the Ka'ba.
Rukū'	ركوع	The position in the prayer in which the head is bent forward with the palms of the hands resting on the knees while the arms are stretched.
Ruqbah	رقبة	A kind of gift forbidden by Islāmic law in which a house is given to someone to live in as long as he lives.
Ruqyah	رقية	Enchanting. A divine speech recited as a means of curing an illness in someone who is sick. For example, to recite al-Fātiḥah or some portions of the Holy Qurān.
Ru'yā	رؤيا	A vision of the Prophets or pious people.

—S—

Ṣā'	صاع	A measure for corn, etc. Equals four (4) Mudds or 2.2 pounds.
Sabā'	سبأ	A province of the country of Yemen. Also, a tribe. The title of 34th Sūra of the Holy Qurān, "The Tribe."
aṣ-Ṣabā	الصبا	Easterly wind.
Ṣabāḥāh	صباحاه	An exclamation indicating an appeal for help.
as-Sab'-ul-Mathānī	السبع المثاني	Sūrat-ul-Fātiḥah, the seven repeated verses.
Ṣābi'	صابى	One who changes his religion. A group of people whose religion is similar to Christianity; however, they claim to practise the religion of Nūḥ (Noah) (A.A.). Their direction of prayer is towards the Southern wind. Some scholars say they are Angel worshippers and others say they are Planet worshippers. (al-Muḥīṭ Dictionary).
Ṣād	صاد	The 14th letter of the Arabic alphabet, the title of the 38th Sūra of the Holy Qurān.
Sa'dān	سعدان	A thorny plant suitable for grazing camels.
Ṣadaqah	صدقه	Anything given in charity, almsgiving.

Ṣadr	صدر	The chief judge, the president.
aṣ-Ṣafā	الصفا	One of the two (2) hills (Ṣafā and Marwah) near the Ka'ba at Mecca to the east. One who performs Ḥajj or 'Umra must walk seven (7) times between these two (2) hills with running between Mīlain-ul-Khaḍarain. This ceremony of Ḥajj is called Sa'ī. See also Sa'ī.
Ṣaff	صفّ	A row in a prayer of congregation. The title of the 61st Sūra of the Holy Qurān.
aṣ-Ṣaf-fāt	الصّفّاة	"Ranged in Ranks," the title of the 37th Sūra of the Holy Qurān.
Ṣafī-ullāh	صفيّ الله	"The Chosen by Allāh," a title given to Prophet Adam (A.A.).
Ṣaḥābī	صحابي	A companion or an associate of Prophet Muḥammad (S.A.A.W.), who saw him during his life.
Ṣāḥib-un-Niṣāb	صاحب النّصاب	One who possesses enough property to be liable to pay Zakāt. Also see Mālik-un-Niṣāb.
Ṣaḥīfah	صحيفة	A booklet, a pamphlet. The revelations given to 'Ibrāhīm (A.A.) and Moses (A.A.).
Ṣaḥīfat-ul-A'māl	صحيفة الاعمال	The book on which deeds are being recorded by the two (2) angels appointed by Allāh (S.W.), to each person. These books will be opened on the Day of Judgement.
Sahm	سهم	An arrow used for drawing lots. An estate allotted to an heir.
Saḥūr	سحور	The meal taken at dawn before the Fajr prayer during the month of Ramaḍān.
Sahū	سهو	Forgetting. Used here this word means forgetting some Rukn of a prayer. For example, how many Rak'āt a person has prayed, in which case he should perform two (2) more prostrations of Sahū.
Sa'ī	سعي	The ceremony of walking seven (7) times between the hills of Ṣafā and Marwa, a requirement of Ḥajj and 'Umra. See aṣ-Ṣafā.
Sā'ibah	سائبة	Any freed person or animal devoted to an idol. A pre-Islāmic concept and tradition which was abandoned by al-Islām.

Saif-ullāh	سيف الله	"The Sword of Allāh." The title given to the famous general of al-Islām, Khālid bin al-Walīd by Prophet Muḥammad (S.A.A.W.).
Sa'īr	سعير	A special section of Hell.
Saiyyid	سيّد	Master. Used for the decendents of Caliph 'Alī.
Saiyyidī	سيّدي	My Master.
Sajdah	سجدة	"Prostration in Prayer" (touching the ground with the forehead, nose, both hands, knees and the tips of the toes), the title of the 32nd Sūra of the Holy Qurān.
aṣ-Sakhrah	الصّخرة	"The Rock". The rock on which stands the Dome of the rock in the sacred Mosque of al-'Aqṣā in Jerusalem, the Mosque of 'Umar.
Sakīnah	سكينة	Tranquility, calmness, peace.
Sal'	سَلع	A well-known mountain in al-Medīna.
Salaf	سَلَف	A sale in which the price is paid at once for the goods to be delivered later. Men of repute in the past generations. Interest free loan. Ancestors.
as-Salām	السّلام	"The Peaceful One," one of the ninty-nine attributes of Allāh (S.W.).
as-Salām-u-'Alaikum	السّلام عليكم	"Peace be upon you." A traditional way of greeting other Muslims in al-Islām. The reply is: "Wa 'Alaikum-as-Salām wa Raḥmatullāh-i-wa Barakātuhū."
Ṣalāt	صلوة	Prayer. The obligatory or Farḍ prayers are to be offered at five (5) fixed times a day after performing Wuḍū or ablution or Tayammum. Also see: Farḍ, Wuḍū, Tayammum.
Ṣalīb	صليب	A cross, a crucufix.
Ṣāliḥ	صالح	"One who is on the right path." The name given to the Prophet of the tribes of 'Ād and Thamūd.
Salsabīl	سلسبيل	A fresh, free-flowing fountain mentioned in the Holy Qurān.
aṣ-Ṣamad	الصّمد	"The Eternal," one of the ninty-nine attributes of Allāh (S.W.).

as-Samī'	السّميع	"The Hearer," one of the ninty-nine attributes of Allāh (S.W.).
Samī-y	سمّي	The one who bears the same name. Used in the holy Qurān regarding Prophet Yaḥyā (John) (A.A.), the son of Zakariya. See H.Q. 19:7.
Samur	سمر	A kind of thorny tree of the desert.
Ṣan'ā'	صنعاء	The capital city of Yemen.
Sanad	سَنَد	A certificate, a document, a warrant. Also, a chain of men who narrated a Ḥadīth of Prophet Muḥammad (S.A.A.W.). The science of chain of narrators is called "Ilm-us-sanad.'
Sanah	سَنَة	A year.
Ṣanam **Pl-'Aṣnām**	صنم- اصنام	An idol made of stone or other materials used for worship.
Saqar	سَقَر	A section of the Hell-fire.
Sariqah	سرقة	Theft, robbery, stealing.
Ṣarf	صرف	A pure sale where gold is exchanged for gold and silver is exchanged for silver, a transaction not allowed in al-Islām.
Ṣarīf	صريف	A place six (6) miles from Mecca.
Ṣarīḥ	صريح	Explicit or clear according to Islāmic law.
Sāriq	سارق	One who steals, a thief.
Sariyyah	سريّة	An army which is not lead by the Commander-in-chief. The army which was sent by the Prophet (S.A.A.W.), without him participating in the battle was called Sariyah.
Ṣaum	صوم	Fasting, during Ramaḍān or otherwise.
Sawā'im	سوائم	Animals which are grazing and for which Zakā' must be paid.
Sawīq	سويق	A kind of dish made of powdered, roasted wheat barley, sugar and dates.
Sha'bān	شعبان	The eighth (8th) month of the Muslim calendar.

S̲haf'	شفع	Term used for Rak'āt performed in pairs or even numbers.
S̲hafā'ah	شفاعة	Recommendation for forgiveness, intercession.
S̲hag̲hār	شغار	A type of marriage common amongst the Arab pagans in which persons exchange their daughters or sisters in marriage without Mahr.
S̲hahādah	شهادة	The confession of a Muslim, the declaration of faith. Evidence, Martyrdom.
S̲hahīd	شهيد	"Martyr, witness," one of the ninty-nine attributes of Allāh (S.W.).
S̲haik̲h	شيخ	A respectable man, a man of authority, a leader, a learned man.
S̲haiṭān	شيطان	The Devil, Satan.
as̲h-S̲hajarah	الشجرة	The tree, a well-known place between Mecca and al-Medīna, under which the Prophet (S.A.A.W.), arranged the fir:t and second pledge of allegiances. See H.Q. 48:18, al-Fatḥ.
S̲hajja	شجّ	Wounds, especially of the head.
as̲h-S̲hakūr	الشّكور	"The Acknowledger," one of the ninty-nine attributes of Allāh (S.W.).
as̲h-S̲hā'm	الشّام	Territory comprising Syria, Palestine and Jordan.
as̲h-S̲hams	الشّمس	"The Sun," the title of the 41st Sūra of the Holy Qurān.
S̲haqq-ul-Qamar	شقّ القمر	"Splitting of the Moon," a miracle of the Prophet (S.A.A.W.).
S̲har'	شرع	Islāmic law. Also see S̲harī'ah.
S̲harāb	شراب	A drink. Usually used for alcoholic and other intoxicating drinks which are forbidden in al-Islām.
S̲harḥ	شرح	Commentary, expounding.
S̲harī'ah	شريعة	Islamic law based on the Holy Qurān, Ḥadīth, Ijmā' and Qiyāṣ.
S̲harṭ	شرط	The pre-conditions of a contract of a marriage, or any other contract.

Shaw-wāl	شوّال	The tenth (10th) month of the Muslim calendar.
Shirk	شرك	Polytheism, idolatry, paganism, to worship others along with Allāh (S.W.). The opposite of Tauḥīd. See Tauḥīd.
Shirāk	شراك	a leather strap.
Shirkah	شركة	A partnership, a contract between two (2) partners or more.
ash-Shu'arā	الشعراء	"The Poets," the title of the 26th Sūra of the Ho Qurān.
Shuf'ah	شفعة	The right of preemption. According to the juris it is the right to own a share of his new partner pro vided that he pays a substantial amount of money for his share. Also, Shuf'ah is the two (2) Rak'āt of Ḍuḥā.
ash-Shūrā	الشّورىٰ	"The Consultation," the title of the 42nd Sūra of the Holy Qurān.
Shurb	شرب	The drinking of alcohol or intoxicants which is forbidden by Islāmic law.
Ṣibghah	صبغة	A dye. The creation of Allāh (S.W.). See H.Q. 2:138, al-Baqarah.
Ṣid-dīq	صدّيق	One who speaks the truth, a sincere lover of the truth. The title given to Abū Bakr (R.A.A.), the first Khalīfah of Prophet Muḥammad (S.A.A.W.).
Sidrat-ul-Muntahā	سدرة المنتهىٰ	"The Lote-tree of the Eternity," the tree in the seventh (7th) heaven whose roots are in the sixth (6th) heaven in Paradise.
Siffīn	صفّين	A battle between the followers of 'Alī (R.A.A.), and the people of (the battle of) Mu'āwiyah at the side of the river of Euphrates in 'Irāq.
Sij-jādah	سجّادة	A small carpet used for prayer, a prayer rug.
Sij-jil	سجّل	The register, the record of a court of justice, the decree.
Sij-jīl	سجّيل	Baked clay. A kind of punishment by Allāh (S.W.). See H.Q. 105:4, al-Fīl.

Sij-jīn	سجّين	A deep pit in which the register of the actions of the wicked people are kept.
Sijn	سجن	Prison, jail.
Silsilah	سلسلة	A chain or series, an unbroken tradition.
Simsār	سمسار	An agent or a broker.
Sīrah	سيرة	The biography of Prophet Muḥammed (S.A.A.W.).
Ṣirāṭ	صراط	A road. Usually used for the bridge that will be laid across the Hell-Fire for the beleivers to pass over on the Day of Judgement.
aṣ-Ṣirāṭ-u-Mustaqīm	الصراط المستقيم	The right path, al-Islām - the religion of truth.
Siwāk	سواك	A piece of a branch or root of a tree called al-'Arāk used as a toothbrush. Also see al-'Arāk.
Siyar	سير	Going in ant manner or pace. The record of man's actions and exploits, the stories of the ancients.
Subḥah	سبحة	The rosary of ninty-nine beads for counting supplications.
Subḥāna	سبحان	Tasbīḥ. Honoring Allāh (S.W.), glorification.
Subḥān-Allāh	سبحان الله	"Holiness to Allāh," to honor Allāh (S.W.), from all that is ascribed to Him.
aṣ-Ṣuf-fah	الصّفة	A shaded place in the Mosque of the Prophet (S.A.A.W.), at al-Medīna where poor people and emigrants used to take shelter.
Ṣūfī	صُوفي	One who gives up all worldly things to seek the pleasure or nearness of Allāh (S.W.).
Suḥūliyah	سحولية	A cotton cloth make in a village in Yemen called Suḥūl used for shrouding the Prophet (S.A.A.W.).
Sukr	سكر	Drunkenness, the state of extreme intoxication.
Ṣulh	صلح	Peace, conciliation, concord.
Sulṭān	سلطان	King, ruler. strength, might.
Sundus	سندس	A kind of silk brocade cloth.

Sun-nah	سنة	A path, a way, a manner of life. All of the traditions and practices of the Prophet (S.A.A.W.), that have become models to be followed by all Muslims.
Sun-nī	سنّي	One of the path, a traditionalist. One who follows the example of Prophet Muḥammad (S.A.A.W.), in all spheres of life.
Sūrah	سورة	A row or series. Strictly used for the chapters of the Holy Qurān.
Sutrah or Sutratu' Muṣal-li	سترة أو سترة المصلّي	That where with anything is concealed or covered. An object like a stick or a spear, ect., that is put in front of a person praying to act as a symbolic barrier between him and the others so that his prayer will not be disturbed or his concentration be distracted.
Suwā'	سواع	An idol mentioned in the Holy Qurān.

—T—

Ṭā'ah	طاعة	Obedience, worship and service to Allāh (S.W.).
Ṭa'ām	طعام	Food.
Ta'aw-wuth	تعوذ	A daily prayer or supplication which means: "I seek refuge with Allāh from the cursed Satan." Also called 'A'ūthu Billāh.
Ṭābah	طابة	Another name for the city of al-Medīna.
Tabat-tal	تبتّل	To retire from the world and to devote one's life to Allāh (S.W.). See H.Q. 73:8.
Tābi'ut-Tābi'īn	تابع التابعين	The follower of the followers. Those who conversed with the companions of the Prophet (S.A.A.W.).
Ṭabīb	طبيب	A Doctor of Medicine, also called Ḥakīm.
Tablīgh	تبليغ	Spreading the teachings of Allāh (S.W.). Delivering the message of al-Islām. Preaching al-Islām.
Tabrīk	تبريك	May Allāh (S.W.) bestow His blessings on you.
Tabūk	تبوك	A valley about 700 miles north of al-Medīna where a military expedition took place against the romans. This battle, which was attended by at least 40,000 people, was the last battle lead by the Pro-

phet (S.A.A.W.) himself. The army was called Jaish-ul-'Usrah. See Jaish-ul-'Usrah.

Tābūt تابوت Noah's Ark. A coffin. The box in which the child Moses was places by his mother from fear of the pharoah on the order of Allāh (S.W.).

Tafsīr تفسير The commentary of the Holy Qurān, and explanation.

at-Taghābun التغابن "Mutual Deceit," the title of the 64th Sūra of the Holy Qurān.

Taghlib تغلب An Arabian tribe which settled in Mesopotamia who professed the Christian faith.

Ṭāghūt طاغوت An idol mentioned in the Holy Qurān. Also, a tyrant.

Ṭā Hā طٰهٰ The title of the 20th Sūra of the Holy Qurān. Also, one of the names of Prophet Muḥammad (S.A.A.W.).

Tahaj-jud تهجد Optional prayers offered at any time between 'Ishā and Fajr.

Taḥāluf تحالف Swearing, the taking of an oath by both parties in a dispute, a state of alliance, a treaty of alliance.

Taḥan-nuth تحنّث Avoiding and obstaining from sin. Worshipping in seclusion.

Ṭahārah طهارة Purification according to Islāmic traditions.

Ṭāhir طاهر Anything in the state of purity.

Tahlīl تحليل The exclamation of saying Lā 'Ilāha 'Illal-lāh, "None has the right to be worshipped but Allāh."

Taḥmīd تحميد The exclamation of saying Al-ḥamd-u-Lil-lāh, "All praises are due to Allāh alone."

Taḥnīk تحنيك A custom of the early Muslims in which a newly born child would be taken to the Prophet (S.A.A.W.), who would chew a piece of date and put part of the morsel in the child's mouth.

Taḥrīf تحريف The alterations in the Holy Torah and the Bible introducted by the Jews and the Christians to suit themselves from time to time.

at-Taḥrīm	التحريم	"The Prohibition," the title of the 66th Sūra of the Holy Qurān.
at-Ṭā'if	الطّائف	A town about 80 kilometers from Mecca which was besieged by the Muslims in the 8th year of Hijra and then raised.
Ṭaiy	طي	A tribe of Jews and Christians who emigrated from Yemen to Najad and became Muslims in 632 A.D.
at-Takāthur	التكاثر	"Multiplying," the title of the 102nd Sūra of the Holy Qurān.
Takbīr	تكبير	Saying Allāh-u-'Akbar, "Allāh is Great." Usually repeated three (3) times.
Takbīrah	تكبيره	A single utterance of Allāh-u-Akbar.
Takbīr-ut-Taḥrīm or 'Iḥrām	تكبيرة التحريم او تكبيرة الاحرام ام	The first Takbīr in the beginning of a regular prayer, said facing the Qibla.
Ṭalāq	طلاق	"Divorce," the title of the 65th Sūra of the Holy Qurān.
Talbiyah	تلبية	Waiting or standing for orders. Saying: "Labbaik, Allāhuma Labbaik," loudly from the beginning to the end of Ḥajj and/or 'Umra, meaning that I am present to respond to your call, O Allāh.
Talmūd	تلمود	The Jewish traditional law.
Tamat-tu'	تمتّع	Reaping the advantage. Performing Ḥajj and 'Umra separately.
Tamjīd	تمجيد	The exclamation, saying: "Allāh is the Most Glorified," "All glory is due to Allāh (S.W.)."
Tanāsukh	تناسخ	The death of an heir before he/she has recieved his/her inheritance. Also, succession, transmigration of souls which are distorted and misguided.
Tanfīl	تنفيل	Looting or plundering in a religious war or battle.
at-Tan'īm	التّنعيم	A place north of Mecca. A Mīqāt where people who are staying in Mecca can go to perform Ghusl, make the intention to perform 'Umra and then return to Mecca to perform 'Umra.

Taqar-rub تقرّب Trying to be near Allāh (S.W.), by various forms of worship.

Taqdīr تقدير Destiny or fate. Predestination, al-Qadar. See al-Qadar.

Taqwā تقوى Purity, abstinence, fear of Allāh (S.W.), piety, righteousness.

Tarāwīḥ تراويح The eight (8) or 20 optional prayers offered after the 'Ishā' prayers during the nights of Ramaḍān. The Tarāwiḥ are to be offered in a mosque or at home, either individually or in a congregation. This was established regularily by Khalīfah 'Umar (R.A.A.).

Tarikah تركة Inheritance, a legacy, a bequest.

aṭ-Ṭāriq الطارق "The Nightcomer," the title of the 86th Sūra of the Holy Qurān.

Tarjī' ترجيع The exclamation, saying: "In-na lil-lāhi wa 'in-nā ilaihi Rāji'ūn," Surely, we belong to Allāh (S.W.), and surely to Him we shall return.

Tarwiyah تروية Giving attention. Satisfying thirst. The eighth (8th) day of Ḥajj.

Taṣaw-wuf تصوف The doctrines of Islāmic mysticism, related to 'Ahluṣ-Ṣuffah. This practice has a fairly sizable group of adherents with some influence. Taṣaw-wuf means the purity of faith and of heart. Some, however, attribute Taṣaw-wuf to the wearing of wool or ragged clothing. It has been promoted as a type of Islāmic Philosophy to which many learned men defend and/or adhere. For example, al-Ḥallāj, 'Ibn 'Arabī, al-Jīlānī, al-Ghazālī and al-Junaid. The word Taṣaw-wuf was not used until the middle of the second century of Hijrah.

Tasbīḥ تسبيح The expression "Subḥān Allāh," meaning: I extol the holiness of Allāh.

Tashah-hud تشهد Testimony. The recitation of the invocation while in Qu'ūd (sitting position) in prayer.

Tashrīq (the days of) تشريق او ايام التشريق Drying flesh in the sun. The 11th, 12th, and 13th days of Thul-Ḥijjah on which animals are sacrificed as an act of worship and obedience to Allāh (S.W.), as performed by 'Ibrāhīm (A.A).

Taslīm تسليم The act at the end of a regular prayer in which one turns one's face to the right and then to the left saying: "Assalām-u-'Alaikum wa Raḥmatullāh," which means may the peace and mercy of Allāh (S.W.) be upon you.

Tasmī' تسميع The expression recited by the 'Imām after rising from Rukū': Sami'a-Allāhu liman ḥamidah," meaning: "Allāh hears him who praises Him."

Tasmiyah تسمية Giving a name, meaning saying Bismillāh or in the Name of Allāh (S.W.). To be used before the commencement of all Sūras, all religious acts or any act whatsoever.

Taṭaw-wu' تطوع Performing all of the Sunnah and Nawāfil acts recommended in the Holy Qurān and the Ḥadīth.

at-Taṭfīf التطفيف "Giving Short Measure," the title of the 83rd Sūra of the Holy Qurān.

Taṭ-hīr تطهير Purifying the impure. For example, washing seven (7) times with water and once with soil if touched by a dog.

Ta'thīr تعذير To repel or censure for offenses not under Ḥadd, which is a diyine statute of legal punishment in accordance with Islāmic Jurisprudence.

Tathwīb تثويب Repeating: "Assalāt-u-khairum-mina-n-naum," meaning that prayer is better than sleep in the morning 'Āthān.

Taubah توبة Asking for forgiveness, to repent. The title of the 9th Sūra of the Holy Qurān.

at-Taubat-un-Naṣūḥ التوبة النصوح Sincere repentance. Asking for forgiveness or repenting of sins from the heart rather than doing lip service. This means: (1) Intention to repent completely from sin. (2) Intention not to go back and repeat the sin again. (3) If the sin was made against a particular individual a direct apology is needed. (4) If the sin was against one of Allāh's rules and regulations, seeking Allāh's forgiveness is necessary. (5) Regretting the sin.

Tauḥīd توحيد Monotheism. Unity of Allāh, one of the fundamental principles of al-Islām. The following three (3) kinds of Tauḥīd are included in the Muslim basic testimony of faith: "Lā 'Ilāha 'Ill-Allāh," None has the right to be worshipped but Allāh. (1) Tauḥīd-ur-Rubūbiyah, Unity of Lordship. To believe that there is only one Allāh for all the universe, our Lord (S.W.). (2) Tauḥīd-ul-'Ulūhiyya, Unity of Worship. To believe that none has the right to be worshipped but Allāh (S.W.). (3) Tauḥīd-al-'Asmā' waṣ-Ṣifāt, Unity of Names and Attributes of Allāh (S.W.). To beleive that: (a)We must not name or qualify Allāh (S.W.), except with what He or His Apostle (S.A.A.W.), has named or qualified Him. (b) None but Allāh (S.W.), can be named or qualified with the names or attributes of Allāh. For example: al-Karīm, ar-Raḥmān, etc. (c) We must confirm all of Allāh's attributes which Allāh (S.W.), has stated in His Book, the Holy Qurān, or mentioned through His Apostle, Muḥammad (S.A.A.W.), without twisting the meaning or giving resemblance to anything created. A fourth kind of Ṭauḥīd is Tauḥīd-al-'Ittibā', Unity of Following Allāh's Apostle Muḥammad (S.A.A.W.). This is included in the second part of the Muslim testimony of faith that states: "Muḥammad-ur-Rasūlullāh," Muḥammad (S.A.A.W.) is Allāh's Apostle and that none has the right to be followed after Allāh's Book or Order, the Holy Qurān but Allāh's Prophet, Muḥammad (S.A.A.W.).

Taujīh **توجية** **Any expression recited before or after Takbir.**

Taurāt **توراة** **The Old Testament, the book of Prophet Moses the Torah.**

Ṭawāf **طواف** **The act of circumambulation or going around the Ka'ba, seven times.**

Ṭawāf-ul-'Ifādah **طواف الإفاضة** **The Ṭawāf around the Ka'ba by the Pilgrims after they have come back from Minā after the tenth (10th) of Thul-Hijja. This is one of the most essential ceremonies of Ḥajj (Rukn).**

Ṭawāf-ul-Wadā' **طواف الوداع** The Ṭawāf that one must perform before leaving Mecca for home.

Ta'wīth **تعويذ** To flee for refuge. A charm or amulet containing written verses from the Holy Qurān worn for protection against evil. It is not recommended in al-Islām.

at-Taw-wāb	التّواب	"The Repenting," one of the ninty-nine attributes of Allāh (S.W.).
Tayam-mum	تيمّم	Intending or proposing a certain act. Usually used for the ablution performed with dust or sand when water is not easily obtainable. Put hands over the clean earth and then pass the palms of each in the back of the other hand, blow off the dust and then pass the hands over the face.
Tazkiyah	تزكية	Purifying. Giving Zakāt. Inquiring the character of a witness.
Tazwīj	تزويج	Joining. A marriage contract.
T̲habḥ	ذبح	The cutting of the throat of an animal in a prescribed manner to make it suitable for Muslims to eat. To make the killing Ḥalāl.
T̲habīḥah	ذبيحة	An animal slaughtered according to Islāmic law. Ḥalāl.
at̲h-Ṭhāhir	الظاهر	"The Evident," one of the ninty-nine attributes of Allāh (S.W.).
Thaiyib	ثيّب	A woman separated from her husband after the first intercourse.
T̲hākir	ذاكر	One who remembers Allāh (S.W.), very much. A reciter of T̲hikr and Qurān.
T̲hanb	ذنب	A crime, a sin, a misdeed.
Thāniyāt-ul-Wadā	ثنيّات الوداع	A place in al-Medīna where Prophet Muḥammad (S.A.A.W.), was first seen while entering the city.
Ṭhann	ظنّ	Opinion, thinking, suspicion.
Tharīd	ثريد	A special dish prepared with meat and bread.
at̲h-T̲hāriyāt	الذاريات	"The Scatterers," the title of the 51st Sūra of the Holy Qurān.
T̲har-rah **Pl-T̲har-rāt**	ذرّة ذرّات	An atom, a very small particle. An ant.
T̲hāt-ul-Jais̲h	ذات الجيش	A place near al-Medīna where a small battle took place.

T͟hāt-un-Niṭāqain ذات النّطاقين "The Two-Belted Woman." a nickname given to 'Asmā', the daughter of 'Abū Bakr (the second K͟halīfah), by Prophet Muḥammad (S.A.A.W.).

T͟hāt-us-Ṣawārī ذات الصّواري The name of a sea battle. It was the first sea battle in al-Islām and was fought during the time of Mu'āwiyah. Refering to Sariyah or pole.

Thaur ثور A well known mountain in Mecca that has a cave in which Prophet Muḥammad (S.A.A.W.) hid himself with 'Abū Bakr (R.A.) during migration to Al-Medīna.

T͟hikr ذكر Remembrance. Recital of the Holy Qurān, mentioning Allāh's names, invocations whether loudly, lowly or mentally to please Allāh (S.W.). The word T͟hikr is mentioned 109 times in the Holy Qurān.

T͟him-mah ذمّة Covenant of protection.

T͟him-mī ذمّي A non-Muslim living under the protection of an Islāmic government and paying the capital tax. See Jizyah.

T͟huhr ظهر The midday or noon prayer.

T͟h-ul-'Arḥām ذوالأرحام Kindred of blood, blood relation.

T͟hul-Fiqār ذوالفقار The name of the sword of Prophet Muḥammad (S.A.A.W.), which he later gave to K͟halīfah 'Alī (R.A.A.) as a gift.

T͟hul-furūḍ ذوالفروض Sharers of the inheritance.

T͟hul-Ḥijjah ذوالحجّة The twelvth (12th) month of the Muslim calendar, the month of Ḥajj

T͟hul-Ḥalaifah ذوالخليفة A place outside al-Medīna, the Mīqāt of the people of al-Medīna and now called Bi'r 'Alī.

T͟hul-Jabīn ذوالجبين The title of the helmet of the Prophet (S.A.A.W.).

T͟hul-Jalāl-wal-'Ikrām ذوالجلال والاكرام "The Lord of Majesty and Generosity," one of the ninty-nine attributes of Allāh (S.W.).

T͟hul-Khalāṣah ذوالخلاصة The Ka'ba al-Yamāniy-ya. A house in Yemen where the idols used to be worshipped which belonged to the tribes of Khat͟h'am and Bajailah.

T̲hulkifl	ذوالكفل	Ezekiel (A.A.), a prophet of Allāh.
Ṭhulm	ظلم	Injustice, wrong-doing, acting tyranically.
Ṭhulmah	ظلمة	Darkness, a period of ignorance, the pre-Islāmic period.
T̲hul-Qa'dah	ذوالقعدة	The eleventh (11th) month of the Muslim calendar.
T̲hul-Qarnain	ذوالقرنين	A great ruler in the past who was a true believer and whose story is mentioned in the Holy Qurān, 18:83.
T̲hū-maḥram	ذومحرم	A male whom a woman can never marry because of a close blood relationship, such as a brother, a father, an uncle, etc. Also, T̲hū-maḥram may refer to her own husband.
T̲hu'n-nūn	ذوالنّون	The title given to Prophet Younus (Jonas) (A.A.).
T̲hur-ri-yah	ذرّية	Offspring, descendents, ancestory.
T̲hu-Ṭuwā	ذو طوى	A well-known well in Mecca.
Ṭībah	طِيبَة	One of the name of the city of al-Medīna.
Tilā'	تلاوع	A kind of alcoholic drink prepared from grapes.
Tilāwah	تلاوة	A reading of the Holy Qurān.
at-Tīn	التين	"The Fig," the title of the 95th Sūra of the Holy Qurān.
Tīn-ul-K̲habal	تين الخبل	The sweat of the people of Hell. This term used frequently in Ḥadīth.
Ṭīrah	طيرة	Levity of the mind, lightness. Ṭīrah is forbidden in Ḥadīth.
Tub-ba'	تُبَّع	A Himayrite Arab tribe mentioned in the Holy Qurān.
Tubbān	تبّان	Shirts that are long enough to cover the knees.
Ṭuhr	طهر	The period of purity of any woman.
Ṭulaqā'	طلقاء	Those persons who embraced al-Islām on the day of the Conquest of Mecca.
at-Ṭūr	الطّور	A mountain mentioned in the Holy Qurān, 2:63.

Ṭuwā	طوى	A sacred valley mentioned in the Holy Qurān, 20:12.

—U—

'Ubūdiyah	عبودية	Slavery.
'Udḥiyah	اضحية	Sacrifice.
al-'Ufuq-ul-A'lā	الافق الاعلى	The Upper Heavens, where Jibrīl was at the time of the revelation to Prophet Muḥammad (S.A.A.W.).
'Uḥud	أحُد	A well-known mountain about three (3) miles north of al-Medīna where one of the greatest battles in Islāmic history took place; after initial setbacks, the Muslims eventually won.
'Ulamā'	علماء	Scholars, learned men, knowledgable men.
'Ulūhiyah	الوهية	Of divine, divinity.
'Ummah	أمّة	A nation, a people, a sect. Usually used to describe the Muslims.
'Ummī	أمّي	An illiterate, an unlettered person.
'Umm-ul-Mu'minīn	أمّ المؤمنين	A title given to the wives of the Prophet (S.A.A.W.), which means The Mother of the Faithful Believers.
'Umm-ul-Qurā	أمّ القرى	A title given to Mecca, meaning The Mother of the Villages.
'Umm-al-Walad	أمّ الولد	A slave woman who begets a child from her master.
'Umrah	عمرة	A lesser ceremony than Ḥajj in which a person comes to Mecca during or out of the season of Ḥajj and performs Ṭawāf and Sa'ī. See also Ṭawāf and Sa'ī.
'Umrā'	أمراء	A synonym of Ruqbā'. See Ruqbā
'Umūmah	أمومة	Maternity, motherhood.
'Uqāb	عقاب	A black eagle.
'Uqbā	عقبى	The end, a reward for good or bad deeds, the Hereafter

'Ūqiyah	اوقية	A weight equal to 38.67 grams.
'Uqūbah	عقوبة	Punishment awarded by the Qāḍī, an authorized Muslim judge.
'Uqūq	عقوق	Disobedience, used especially in Islāmic terminology with regard to disobedience to parents.
'Uqūqul-Wālidain	عقوق الوالدين	Disobedience or disrespect for parents.
'Urfuṭ	عرفط	A tree which produces Maghāfir. See Maghāfir.
'Urs	عرس	A marriage celebration, an anniyersary celebration.
'Urwah	عروة	Literally means buttonhole. Figuratively or symbolicly means the strong tie. See H.Q. 2:256.
'Ushr	عشر	One tenth (1/10th) of the yield of land given to Bait-ul-Māl for public assistance. See Bait-ul-Māl.
'Uṣūl	أُصول	Roots. The fundamentals of al-Islām.
'Uthr	عذر	An excuse.
al-'Uzzā	العزى	An idol worshipped by the pre-Islāmic Arab pagans which is mentioned in the Holy Qurān, 53:19.

—W—

Wad-d	ودّ	An idol, idolatry, an idolater.
Wadī'ah	وديعة	A thing put down, a deposit.
al-Wadūd	الودود	"The Loving One," one of the ninty-nine attributes of Allāh (S.W.).
Waḥdāniyah	وحدانيه	Unity or oneness of Allāh (S.W.). See Tauḥīd.
al-Wah-hāb	الوهاب	"The Bestower," one of the ninty-nine attributes of Allāh (S.W.).
Waiḥaka	ويحك	An exclamation: May Allāh (S.W.) be merciful to you.
Wailaka	وَيلَك	An exclamation: Woe be upon you.
Wāi'th	واعظ	The preacher, the 'Imām, the one who recites the Khuṭbah on Friday.

Wajh	وجه	Face. Presence of Allāh (S.W.).
Wājib	واجب	Something that is obligatory according to Islāmic law.
al-Wājid	الواجد	"The Finder," one of the ninty-nine attributes of Allāh (S.W.).
Wakālah	وكالة	The agency. An embassy. An attorneyship.
Wakīl	وكيل	An agent. An embassador. An attorney.
al-Wakīl	الوكيل	"The Guardian," one of the ninty-nine attributes of Allāh (S.W.).
Walā'	ولاء	Friendship, proximity, kinship. A good relationship between a freed slave and his/her former master.
Walhān	ولهان	The divil or demon troubling people during ablution.
Walī	ولي	A saint, a holy man.
al-Walī	الولي	"The Helper," one of the ninty-nine attributes of Allāh (S.W.).
Wālī	والي	Governor, prince, the ruler of a country. Allāh (S.W.).
Walīmah	وليمه	A wedding feast given on the morning or noon after the Nikāḥ.
Waqf	وقف	Property assigned for the service of Allāh (S.W.). An endowment.
Wāqi'ah	واقعه	The inevitable. Usually used to refer to the Day of Judgement. The title of the 56th Sūra of the Holy Qurān.
Waqṣ	وقص	Property on which Zakāt is due. Charity to be paid in the period between paying the Zakāt of one year and the Zakāt of the next year.
al-Wārith	الوارث	"The Heir," one of the ninty-nine attributes of Allāh (S.W.).
Wars	ورس	A kind of perfume.

al-Wāsi'	الواسع	"The Capacious," one of the ninty-nine attributes of Allāh (S.W.).
Waṣīyah **Pl-Waṣāyā**	وصية وصايا	Wills and testaments.
Wasīlah	وسيلة	A mediator. Nearness. The highest place in Paradise, as explained by Prophet Muḥammad (S.A.A.W.) in Ṣaḥīh Muslim.
Wāsiṭah	واسطة	A mediator, an agent, one who intervenes, a broker.
Waswasah	وسوسة	Inspiring, suggesting. The mechanism of the devil's work.
Wa'ṭh	وعظ	A sermon, a Khuṭbah.
Waṭhīfah	وظيفة	A scholarship, a pension, a stipend, a daily lesson, a revenue. Also, certain prayers and supplications ascribed by the Prophet (S.A.A.W.).
Wazīr	وزير	A minister.
Wiṣāl	وصال	Fasting continuously for more than one day in a row other than during the month of Ramaḍān.
Witr	وتر	An odd number. Optional, odd numbered Rak'āt prayers performed after 'Ishā' in which Du'ā'-al-Qunūt is recited. Usually, three (3) Rak'āt are performed, but any odd number is acceptable: 1, 5, etc.
Wuḍū'	وضوء	Ablution made before saying the prayers in the traditional manner as described in Ḥadīth.
Wujūd	وجود	An existance.
Wuqūf	وقوف	Standing. Standing in prayer. The ceremonies of Ḥajj performed in the plains of 'Arafāt.

—Y—

Yad-ul-lāh	يدالله	The Hand of Allāh (S.W.), a figurative expression.
Yaghūth	يغوث	An idol mentioned in the Holy Qurān. 71:23.
Yahūd	يهود	Plural of Yahūdī. The Jews.

Yājūj-wa-Mājūj	ياجوج وماجوج	Gog and Magog, the two (2) tribes of ancient people who lived by the Ma'rib Dam in the Yemen.
Yalamlam	يلملم	The Mīqāt of the people coming from Yemen for Ḥajj.
Yamāmah	يمامة	An eastern province of Ḥijāz.
al-Yaman	اليمن	Yemen, a country located to the south of Saūdī 'Arabia.
Yamīn	يمين	An oath, a vow. The right.
al-Yaqīn	اليقين	Belief, sure knowledge. The certainty.
Yā Sīn	يٰس	The title of the 36th Sūra of the Holy Qurān.
Ya'-sūb	يعسوب	The King of the Bees, a title given to Kh̲alīfah 'Alī (R.A.A.).
Yathrib	يثرب	An old name for al-Medīna, changed to Madīnat-un-Nabī by Prophet Muḥammad (S.A.A.W.). See Madīnat-un-Nabī.
Yatīm	يتيم	Orphan. A title given to Prophet Muḥammad (S.A.A.W.), because he was born an orphan.
Yaum	يوم	A day.
Yaum-ud-Dīn	يوم الدّين	The Day of Judgement.
al-Yaum-ul-'Ākh̲ir	اليوم الآخر	The Last Day. Another name for the Day of Judgement.
Yaum 'Ash̲ūrā'	يوم عاشورة	The tenth (10th) day of Muḥar-ram. It is a big day of celebration in the Jewish faith. According to Ḥadīth, however, the Prophet (S.A.A.W.) declared that we, the Muslims, are closer to Prophet Moses (A.A.) than the Jews and said: "If I live to the next year, I am going to fast the 9th and 10th of Muharram."
Yaum-ul-Faṣl	يوم الفصل	The Day of Severing. Another name for the Day of Judgement.

—Z—

az-Zabāniyah	الزبانيه	The Guards, the angels who are in charge of Hell.
Zabūr	زبور	A booklet, a pamphlet. The psalms of Prophet David (A.A.).
Zafīr	زفير	The groan or noise of Hell.
Zaḥf	زحف	An army, a swarming multitude, a force ready to fight.
Zāhid	زاهد	Abstinent, continent, an ascetic. A person who does not concern himself with the worldly matters, especially the ephemeral of this world.
Zā'ir	زائر	A pilgrim or visitor to Prophet Muḥammad's (S.A.A.W.) Mosque in al-Medīna.
Zakāt	زكاة	Obligatory Charity. Literally means purification. The amount of Zakāt is certain fixed percentage (2.5) to be paid on all valuables and property which has been held or is in one's possession for one full year. Zakāt is to be paid yearly for the benefit of the needy and the poor in the Muslim community. Zakāt is Farḍ as it is one of the five (5) major pillars of al-Islām and is a major economic means for establishing social justice, prosperity and social security within the Muslim community and government.
Zakāt-ul-Fiṭr	زكاة الفطر	An obligatory Ṣadaqah to be given before the prayer of 'Īd-ul-Fiṭr. It is Farḍ for every fasting Muslim. In a household, the father is responsible for the payment of all those who fasted in his family.
Zam-Zam	زمزم	The sacred well within the confines of the Holy Mosque in Mecca from which 'Ismā'īl and Hājar drank. The water from the well of Zam-Zam is considered to be sacred and healthy and is taken by millions of pilgrams during Ḥajj and 'Umra as well as other times.
Zaqqūm	زقوم	A tree with exceedingly bitter fruit described in the Holy Qurān. See H.Q. 37:62.

al-Zilzāl	الزلزال	"The Earthquake", the title of 99th Sūra of the Holy Qurān.
Zinā	زنى	Adultery, the punishment for which, according to the Islāmic law, is Rajm, i.e. stoning to death.
Zindīq	زنديق	A person beyond cure as far as his disbelief is concerned.
Ziyārah	زيارة	A visit to the Holy Places, Mosque at Mecca, Medīna or Jerusalem.
Zuhd	زهد	A religious life, abstinence.
az-Zukhruf	الزخرف	"Gilding", the title of 43rd Sūra of the Holy Qurān.
az-Zumar	الزمر	"Troops", the title of 39th Sūra of the Holy Qurān.

REFERENCES

*1. 'Alī, A. Yousuf, THE HOLY QUR'ĀN Commentary & Translation with Arabic Text, 1939, Sheikh Muhammad Ashraf, Lahore (Pakistan).

2. Bāqī, M. Fuad 'Abdul, CONCORDANCE OF THE HOLY QUR'ĀN Reproduced, 1945, Dar-ul-Kutab al-Misriyya, Beirut (Lebanon).

*3. Hughes, T. P., DICTIONARY OF ISLĀM, Reproduced, 1965, Reference Book Publishers, (USA).

*4. Khān, Dr. Muḥammad Muḥsin, ṢAḤĪḤ-AL-BUKHĀRĪ, Arabic-English, The meaning of the translation of, 1977, Kazi Publications, Chicago (USA).

5. Muslim, Imām, ṢAḤĪḤ MUSLIM Commentary by Imām an-Nawwāwī, 2nd Print 1972, Dar Ihya Turath, Beirut (Lebanon).

*6. Wehr, Hans, ARABIC-ENGLISH DICTIONARY Edited by J. M. Cowan, 1976, Spoken Languages Services, (USA).